T0208019

IN GOD'S GRIP

CARL DAMBMAN

WESTBOW
PRESS®
A DIVISION OF THOMAS NELSON
& ZONDERVAN

WestBow Press books may be ordered through booksellers or by contacting:

WestBow Press
A Division of Thomas Nelson & Zondervan
1663 Liberty Drive
Bloomington, IN 47403
www.westbowpress.com
844-714-3454

ISBN: 978-1-6642-7335-1 (sc)
ISBN: 978-1-6642-7336-8 (hc)
ISBN: 978-1-6642-7337-5 (e)

Library of Congress Control Number: 2022913700

Print information available on the last page.

WestBow Press rev. date: 9/1/2022

RECOMMENDATIONS

"As a football coach, I have had tremendous respect for wrestlers since I was a student at the University of Minnesota. My close friend, Tom Lamphere, longtime chaplain for the Vikings, was part of a pioneering team of Christian wrestlers who used their athletic skills as a bridge for ministry into countries behind the Iron Curtain. *In God's Grip* shares the true story of that team, and of others, who joined in bringing the Good News to people in the former Soviet Bloc during the hard days of communist rule." –**Tony Dungy**, Super Bowl-winning NFL head coach, NBC sports analyst, and New York Times best-selling author.

"While Jacob in the Bible wrestled *with* God, Carl Dambman wrestled *for* God!! Olympian Carl and the Athletes in Action wrestling team helped change the world through competitive events and the Gospel! *In God's Grip* tells the story of how Carl's team used sports as a platform for worldwide evangelism, especially in Communist countries." –**Josh D. McDowell**, Author.

"As a two-time Super Bowl Champion, I had tremendous opportunity for sharing my faith with sports fans and encouraging other athletes. I have personally witnessed how sports ministry provides an avenue into the hearts of adults and children all over the world. I met Carl Dambman at the 1988 Olympics in Korea, and we began a friendship that has lasted more than three decades. Carl is a pioneer of global sports ministry, who uses his platform as a world class wrestler to proclaim his faith, and to help others find and grow in theirs. Having seen Carl's influence on young athletes in Russia and other parts of the world, I heartily commend to you *In God's Grip* for its inspiration as a true story of God's power working through athletes to spread the Gospel." –**Norm Evans**, former president of Pro Athletes Outreach (PAO), and all-pro offensive lineman.

"In 1972, in a media-hyped Summit Series between Canada and the Soviets in Moscow, I scored the series-winning goal with 34 seconds left to play. That moment was later voted by the Canadian Press as "the sports moment of the century". Twenty years later, I was invited to speak on a sports-ministry tour organized by AIA in Moscow, with Carl Dambman as the team leader. In that city where my team had won a prize that perishes, I was able to speak to athletes and others of a much greater prize that never perishes. Since that time, I have continued to witness the high-impact results of sports ministry. I commend to you *In God's Grip*, which tells not only the exciting story of sports missionaries, but also provides wisdom for how athletes can better negotiate the pressures of championship level sports." –**Paul Henderson**, Former NHL and Team Canada hockey player.

"Since I began working with the NBA in 1965, I have seen the Gospel blanket the world of sport. Carl Dambman is one of the earliest pioneers of this initiative, leveraging his platform as a heavyweight Olympic wrestler to mentor and disciple many athletes in Russia and other nations. *In God's Grip* is the thrilling account of a quiet, gentle giant who, like Jacob, wrestled with God. And they both won." –**George Toles**, Former NBA Stadium Announcer for the Detroit Pistons and Seattle Supersonics, and Founder of *His Deal*.

"Carl Dambman has been a faithful pioneer of sports ministry outreach, and an inspiration to all who have ever met him. *In God's Grip* is a window into how the Lord has empowered Carl and others to use sports as a way to reach many for Jesus in lands once considered "closed". Reading this book will bring you into the actual history of men and women whose continual Gospel efforts have been blessed by God to enhance and expand the Church. Thank you, Carl, for your faithfulness in the missionary work the Lord has called you to." –**Dr. Greg Linville**, Doctorate of Ministry, Director at Church Sports & Recreation Ministry.

"Carl Dambman is a big man with a big heart. God has used his friendly and outgoing nature to open people's hearts to the Gospel in some of the most difficult places in the world." –**Greg Hicks**, Author of *In His Grip*, Pan American Wrestling Champion, Two time World Championship USA team member, Radio Host and businessman.

"I met and roomed with Carl at the 1998 Winter Olympics in Japan, and I am familiar with the history of God's faithfulness toward him and his wife, Noreen, as they ventured by faith into parts of the world where most of us would not choose to go. God has caused His light to shine upon and through them for the increase of the Gospel among many. I am excited about this book, which details their journeys and how Christ has shepherded them through it all." –**Mike Buchanan**, AIA staff member since 1990 and author of *More Than That*.

"*In God's Grip* relates the true story of brave men and women who took up the challenge of sharing their faith in distant lands. In reading these stories, you will walk with the Dambmans and others through times of joy, difficulty, tragedy, and humor. You will read about unique experiences of God's power working to spread the Good News of Jesus Christ through faithful servants across language barriers, cultural and governmental resistance, and through endless days of training, travel, competition, and bearing witness. In 1967, I was the first wrestler to join the newly forming Athletes in Action, and more than a half-century later, I rejoice to look back over what God has done through the faith and sacrifice of AIA missionaries such as Carl and Noreen Dambman." –**John Klein**, first AIA wrestler, and staff member since 1967, also a current member of the Global Events Team.

"Having served in Eurasian sports ministry in recent years, my colleagues and I are aware that we stand on the shoulders of ministry pioneers like Carl and his teammates. Having counted the costs, they followed the calling of the Lord Jesus and blazed a trail for the Gospel behind the Iron Curtain. If there are modern-day apostles, Carl Dambman and his pioneering teammates have been exactly that to the sports-ministry world of Eurasia." –**Roger D. Lipe**, Fellowship of Christian Athletes Staff for twenty-five years, author, and trainer in character coaching.

"Carl's reputation in ministry through sport is legendary across the former Soviet Union. When he and I began our ministry in Russia in the early 1990s, there was no manual of strategies on how to bring the Gospel to Russians using sport. We knocked on a lot of doors, prayed about where God was leading us, and through sport brought the Gospel into schools, prisons, sport clubs and orphanages. During Soviet times, most evangelical churches considered taking part in sport to be a sin. By consistently working in partnership with churches across Russia, we helped their leaders understand that sport was not only not sinful, but could be used to reach men and youth." –**Steve Barrett**, 1977 NCAA wrestling champion at Oklahoma State University, and Carl's 20-year ministry partner in the former Soviet Bloc.

"Carl Dambman is the grandfather of sports ministry in the regions of the former Soviet Union. So many people in those areas believed that *Christianity* was for weak and uneducated people, and many in the churches believed that *sport* was sinful. God used Athletes in Action to change people's thinking on both of those points, and to combine sport and faith for an explosive outreach of evangelism and discipleship." –**Tom Merchant**, staff member with Missionary Athletes International, and a partner in Eurasian sports ministry since 1991.

"Carl and his AIA Teammates have been an important part of USA Wrestling since the 1970s. They pioneered sports ministry in the Soviet Bloc, as well as many times helping serve the USA teams competing in Europe and beyond. *In God's Grip* shares how the Total Athlete provides a strong spiritual foundation for sport and life." –**Rich Bender**, Executive Director, USA Wrestling, USA Olympic Committee.

DEDICATION

This book is dedicated to my parents, Walt and Jayne Dambman, and to my wife Noreen's parents, Bob and Norma Berg.

I also dedicate this book to the men and women who partnered with us in the pioneering work of sports ministry in countries behind the Iron Curtain.

ACKNOWLEDGEMENTS

I want to acknowledge the following:

My faithful and beloved wife, Noreen. You wanted to be a missionary before I did.

Our supporters. You have been an important part of our lives, encouraging us through your prayers, your giving, and your friendships.

My wrestling coaches. You saw the potential, and you helped develop me to be a good athlete and a better person.

Campus Crusade for Christ® (Cru®), and Cru's sports ministry, *Athletes in Action*®. Your vision of the Great Commission through the platform of sports enabled me to travel the world and share the Good News of Jesus Christ.

The influence of Bill Bright and Bud Hinkson, along with Josh McDowell and Paul Eshleman. Dr. Bright, you challenged me to come and help fulfill the Great Commission, and to pray for the people in the Soviet Union. Bud, you challenged me to move to Europe for ministry behind the Iron Curtain. Josh, you provided an example through serving, speaking, and writing. Paul, you inspired me with your incredible talents in developing evangelistic sports videos and *The Jesus Film*®.

Our teammates, sports ministry partners, and other missionaries. Also, those who contributed in so many different ways, whose names would fill a book if I were to list each of you.

My writing team, Patrick and Donnalee Griffin. I came to you with a spark, and you fanned it into a flame. You encouraged me to persevere, and together we got the work done.

My editors, Kathy Harl and Melanie Rose, and all of the others who contributed time and expertise toward helping me finalize this project.

My publisher, Westbow Press, a self-publishing division of Thomas Nelson and Zondervan. I am grateful for your professionalism and your values of honoring God and serving others.

CONTENTS

Foreword...xv

Introduction.. xvii

Prologue...xix

Chapter 1   The Early Years 1

Chapter 2   Athletes in Action..8

Chapter 3   Noreen... 17

Chapter 4   Mexico, Iran, and Bulgaria..26

Chapter 5   On the Move...36

Chapter 6   Vienna...42

Chapter 7   If Only I Could Remember My Keys! 50

Chapter 8   Zakopane 60

Chapter 9   Wrestling and Witnessing..66

Chapter 10   Germany 74

Chapter 11   Tear Down This Wall!..83

Chapter 12   Moscow 92

Chapter 13   Highs and Lows 103

Chapter 14   The Gospel and Taekwondo!?! 111

Chapter 15   Our Children Move to the USA 119

Chapter 16   Major Changes 133

Chapter 17   Back in the USA.. 141

Afterword 149

Appendix A   Chapter By Chapter Application 151

Appendix B   Basics of the Christian Walk.................................... 159

Appendix C   Ministry Organizations... 160

Appendix D   Recommended Books 162

Appendix E   Freedom In Christ 164

About the Author 167

FOREWORD

In the Autumn of 1974, at a team gathering near State College, Pennsylvania, I noticed the newcomer, heavyweight prospect Carl Dambman, falling way behind the rest of us as we ran up a steep hill during a training exercise. As a wrestler-coach, I did not feel so confident that Carl was going to be a great asset. Yet here I am, almost a half-century later, writing the Foreword to his book!

As an Olympic athlete, I pushed my body very hard. My desire as a coach was that the wrestlers I coached would learn to do the same. Carl was one of those who did. As was made clear in a later interview with Sports Illustrated, my motivation was "God's love, rather than a desire to fight." As that article accurately reported, the men with Athletes in Action "have committed themselves to a mission for spreading the word of God, and utilize their athletic talent as a means to carry out that mission." During that 1974 weekend gathering, I saw that Carl Dambman wanted to offer his athletic talents to Christ for spreading the Gospel, and to pursue excellence in sports as a way of honoring the Lord. I knew that if he submitted to the rigor of our spiritual and physical training, he would do well with our traveling sports team.

Carl did more than just *well*. On the mat, he helped our team to victory after victory, but more importantly, he grew spiritually and helped AIA to pioneer sports ministry in forbidden lands behind the Iron Curtain. During his active wrestling career, he shared the Gospel and his personal testimony with tens of thousands of people around the world. I could write a full book just on my memories of our times in training camps and tournaments in countries like Hungary, Poland, and Czechoslovakia, where Carl was the guy on our team who smuggled in Bibles and Christian literature.

For most people, hiding literature inside of luggage might not seem like a big deal, but my brother Ben and I had firsthand experience with the communist KGB hunting for Bibles. One time in 1976, we were at a wrestling event in the Soviet Republic of Georgia, with a box of Bibles in our room. One day the KGB checked the room of a teammate next to us. They never did find the Bibles, but that whole experience was scary. On that same trip, after being told the KGB was coming after us, we dropped the few remaining Bibles off a moving train (to this day I wonder who God directed to find them!). My point is that, during the days of communist rule, being the guy who smuggled in Bibles was no small sacrifice, and on our many occasions of crossing borders into those countries, Carl was the guy who volunteered to take the risk.

In this book, what you are going to read about Carl Dambman and others from Athletes in Action helping to pioneer sports ministry worldwide is easily verified by many sources and witnesses. In January of 1991, on a visit to Moscow, I was impressed to see his willingness to step out and take the risks of pioneering Christian sports ministry in the nerve center of atheistic communism. In the sport of wrestling, you have to be zoned in because it is just you and the guy on the mat, and Carl maintained this same focus and courage in ministry. I saw him show that fearlessness in competition, and also in his transitioning from an active wrestler into an international trailblazer using our sport as a tool for ministry.

As Carl's former coach, workout partner, and long-time ministry teammate, I commend *In God's Grip* to you as a true story of God's provision and leading of those He calls, even "to the ends of the earth." –**John Peterson**, Gold and Silver Olympic Medalist, three-time World Cup Champion, AIA staff member since 1973.

INTRODUCTION

Since the mid-1990s, my brother-in-law, Charles, and other friends, have encouraged me to write my story of how God used sports to pioneer ministry in Eastern Europe and the former Soviet Union. The idea for writing my story became a reality during the travel restrictions brought on by the pandemic. Unable to leave my home area near Seattle, I was asked to write the Foreword to a book by a longtime friend, Bill Shubin, who introduced me to a professional writing team. A couple months later, I did my first interview with the writers, answering questions and just talking about my life experiences.

It was quite a journey, walking back through the years, reliving the times of celebration and struggle, reflecting on what I have seen and felt, what I have learned, and what God has accomplished. Above all, working on the book has helped me to appreciate the amazing faithfulness of God who so caringly leads and provides, and who always fulfills His promise to open doors and to never leave nor forsake us.

You will read of my spiritual growth through "the thrill of victory and the agony of defeat." You will also read the history of how God used a handful of wrestlers, with our wives at our sides, to go behind the Iron Curtain and pioneer sports ministries that would join a global network of partnerships working on every continent to spread the Gospel.

When four of us from AIA moved to Austria, with our families in 1979, we had no playbook for how to build national sports ministries in Eastern Europe and the Soviet Union. God used our credentials as Olympic and world-class wrestlers to get us into those countries with access to athletes who for all of their lives had been told that faith in God was for fools and for people who are weak. God enabled us to help change their ideas about that! Coaches and sports leaders for the national teams in communist countries like Poland, Hungary, Czechoslovakia, Ukraine, and even Russia, opened doors for us to train with their teams, giving us the access we needed for sharing with athletes and others the Good News about a personal, saving relationship with the Lord Jesus Christ.

I want readers to find *In God's Grip* interesting, and to gain inspiration and practical wisdom from the stories of God's loving faithfulness. I am also excited about the encouraging stories, which will be available on our website, from others who have been with us over the many years.

Please join me on this missionary adventure, from the suburbs of Philadelphia to lands as far as Siberia, China, Central Asia and South Africa, and see the amazing faithfulness of God who provides, cares for, and leads, sometimes in the most surprising of ways.

PROLOGUE

They came after me. In the wrestling area of the Tashkent Arena in Uzbekistan, an official suddenly approached and demanded to see my papers. I complied, and from there he escorted me to the office of the security chief. Along the way, I was able to send out a text to my team leader, Reid Lamphere, letting him and the others know my situation, and for them to "be careful."

Coming into the office, I saw the chief sitting at his desk, with my wrestling colleague Valera in a nearby chair looking at me with a concerned and apologetic expression. I did my best with body language to assure Valera that we would get through this okay, even though I really was anxious about the outcome. As an American, probably the worst that could happen to me was getting thrown out of the country, but my bigger concern was for the nationals and other non-Americans working with us.

That was September of 2014. I had met up in Central Asia with several teammates from Athletes in Action, for outreach during the Wrestling World Championships. There were four of us who had worked together in ministry since the 1970s, and we shared the deep bond of brotherly friendship that comes with decades of history. In the capital of Tashkent, a gangster-turned-Christian named Rashid, our main national for AIA sports ministry in Uzbekistan, arranged for our lodging, food, and transportation. We had a great time fellowshipping with Rashid and other locals serving in ministry, with all of us rejoicing to see God's blessing on the work in that part of the world.

A top priority in countries with cultural and/or political hostility toward the Gospel was to protect the locals and their ministries. On that occasion, before starting the outreach, we had gathered the ministry team in the courtyard of a hotel, explaining we had brought sports-ministry DVDs and other resources in several languages, including

Russian and Uzbek. Rashid gave some cultural tips and emphasized how everyone needed to be very careful when offering someone a DVD. Also, we had agreed if anyone got into trouble, I would be the fall guy. Reid was clear in instructing them, "If anyone in authority asks where you got the DVDs, tell them *Carl Dambman* gave them to you."

On our third day, Valera, a wrestling coach from Moldova, was spotted giving away a DVD inside the arena. He was quickly detained and interrogated by the authorities. When asked where he had gotten the DVDs, he did exactly as we had instructed, telling the authorities he received them from an American named Carl Dambman.

Now, with both of us surrounded by security in an office out of sight from our teammates, the chief waved a DVD contemptuously and said, "Don't you know this is against our laws?" I told him I had no intention of breaking any laws, and that, "I have been an Olympic Chaplain in Sochi, and have also served as a chaplain at the University Games in Kazan, Russia, so it is normal for me to have spiritual resources." He turned to his computer and pushed some buttons. After getting confirmation on my chaplaincy claim, he turned back to me and said, "But why do you have Christian DVDs in the Uzbek language? We regard this as a threat to our nation." I had to think quickly, and God showed me favor. I said, "Sir, these DVDs are of wrestlers talking about their faith, and since your country has some of the best wrestlers in the entire world, it would be insulting to Uzbekistan if we did not have DVDs in your national language."

The chief squinted his eyes, like he felt there was a problem somewhere in my answer, but he could not quite put a finger on it. For the next three hours, Valera and I endured a grilling of harshly worded questions, but God gave us wisdom for patience and soft answers. Finally, the chief conferred with a couple of his guys, and then he said, "We want to take you to our superiors for more questioning." At that point I slightly stiffened my face and said, "I will not leave this building without first speaking to someone from the U.S. Embassy."

The chief's facial expression showed my statement had put a crack in his confidence. He realized I had plenty of international experience, and as an American I would utilize my rights. After a minute, he said, "Okay, if you will just sign a form acknowledging that we confiscated the DVDs, we will let you go with no further questioning." I nodded, and one of his guys promptly handed me a clipboard with a form. I carefully read the document, signed it, then stood up and left, with Valera following close behind. We were in a country that saw our faith as a threat to national security, and although four of us were Americans, we were a long way from home. Two days later, as our plane lifted off from Tashkent, we breathed a sigh of relief while continuing to pray for the safety of those we had left behind.

Doing ministry in lands not friendly to America or the Gospel had been my business since moving to Europe in 1979. With a small team of athletes and our courageous, self-sacrificing wives, we had used our credentials as world class wrestlers to get into countries behind the Iron Curtain. We did go there to wrestle on the mats, but our greater wrestling match was spiritual. As Americans, we knew we stood little chance of physical harm or "disappearance," but we *always* needed to be mindful of the safety of the nationals who opened their hearts to the testimony of Jesus. We walked that tightrope of courage and caution, and the following stories in this book are a testimony to the Scripture which says,

> *"If the Lord had not been on our side...they would*
> *have swallowed us alive." (Psalms 124:2-3)*

CHAPTER ONE

The Early Years

"'For I know the plans I have for you,' declares the Lord,
'plans to prosper you to give you hope and a future.'"
(JEREMIAH 29:11)

L ooking out through a window into the scenes of my history, I see God's plan for my life first taking shape in the seventh grade. Seated at a table beside an empty chair in the school cafeteria, making the most I could from a thirty-five-cent lunch, a sudden movement drew my eyes to the right. I turned and looked at the rock-jaw face of our gym teacher, Mr. Long. He wore a slight smile and stared straight into my eyes.

"Hi, Carl," he said, settling into the chair while keeping his focus on me. I nodded respectfully while chewing on my lunch. Mr. Long waited for me to swallow, and then he said, "Carl, you are a good athlete. What are your plans for the winter sports?"

I looked away for a second, narrowing my eyes in thought, then I turned back to him and said, "I am thinking about basketball."

He paused a moment, puckering his lips and nodding, like he was really thinking about my answer. Then he leaned his face just a bit closer and said, "Did you know this school is not that great in basketball, but we have not lost a *wrestling* match in three years?"

"Wrestling?" I said, tilting my face like I had just heard some strange new idea.

"Wrestling," he repeated, pulling back his head as though he had just said something profound. Then he reached out and clapped a hand on my shoulder as he zeroed in with his pitch. "Carl, I really want you to be on the wrestling team. We need the *best* athletes in the school."

He could have been a great car salesman. At least, he sure knew how to make a twelve-year-old boy feel special and wanted. Until that day, I do not recall having ever thought seriously about wrestling, but I told him, "Okay, I'll join."

Little did I know...

On the wrestling team under Coach Long, I realized early on that I had some talent for this sport. I also had my first example of what I would come to believe a coach should embody, an instructor of life skills along with athletics. I had an excellent role model at home—my father, a war hero from the beaches of Normandy who brought a kind, caring, supportive presence. Yes, life at home in the suburbs of Philadelphia was good, and the upbringing provided by my parents laid a strong foundation for character and principle, but God used Coach Long to point my face toward the future He had designed.

In my first two years, I was learning the sport, and by the time I reached the ninth grade, I had grown from the 125-pound weight class to 154, and was made co-captain of our team. We had gone undefeated during my first two years, but we lost the second meet in my final year, breaking our streak of fifty-four consecutive wins. As a co-captain, even though I had won my own match, I felt I had let down the school and the community. Right there in the gym I started crying.

Many years later I would see a three-time Olympic gold medalist, Aleksandr Karelin, lose out on his fourth gold in a stunning upset by an American heavyweight. After that loss in the 2000 Sydney Olympics, I would hear Karelin talk in an interview of how empty he felt after "disappointing my country." In sports there is a saying that, "You are only as good as your last results," and at age 14 I was years away from capturing the wisdom that my real worth is not in sport, but in Jesus Christ.

In September of 1965, I started at Upper Darby High School (UDHS), the same school my parents graduated from in 1939. They had a strong wrestling program with really good coaches, Art McCall and Ken Barr. Coach Barr was a serious Christian involved in a ministry called *Young Life*, and he did his best to teach us to build our athletic skills on a spiritual foundation.

As the years passed, I continued to physically outgrow most of the boys in my age group. By September of 1966, I showed up for my junior year weighing 240 and feeling strong. As a heavyweight, this meant I was the last guy on the mat after a dozen previous matches. A win or a loss for a team often comes down to the last match, and on the many occasions when the outcome for my team depended on my performance, I walked away the hero. The downside was I poured too much of my identity into my results in competition, even though I had a coach who tried to teach me better. I was hearing Coach Barr's wisdom with my mind, but I was not gripping it and pulling it into my heart. As a kid growing up in a Christian home, I attended church each Sunday with my family and tried to be a good person, but that was about the extent of my understanding of Christianity. What I really loved, and where I got the most joy and acceptance, was sports.

All in all, those high school years were a good time, but as my senior year drew toward a close, I had no clear idea of what I wanted to do with my life. Actually, I had not given much serious thought to the long-term, until a combination of events and challenges in the months before graduation put me in a more reflective mood.

In March of my senior year, I got beat in the district championship tournament, which I had been expected to win. To work so hard, to get so far, and to lose, was not an easy thing for me to shake off, and I knew I needed to root my ideas about who I am in something deeper than winning a championship. Then, not long after that loss, my girlfriend broke up with me. She was the first girl I had a serious relationship with, and the rejection came as a painful shock. In April, my grandfather Walter C. Dambman, Sr. died. Although I did not know him well because he lived in another state, it hurt to lose him, and it raised my awareness of mortality and the uncertainties of life.

One weekend in April, a few days after my eighteenth birthday, I went to a church retreat. Getting ready to graduate from high school, I had head knowledge about the Bible and who Jesus is, but I needed a personal relationship with Him. One night at the retreat, after the pastor had given a message and the usual mingling and fellowship was going on, I stepped outside for some time alone.

After walking a short distance in a tree studded area, I came to a clearing by a creek and sat on a flat stone. From a few feet away, the splash of rippling water mixed with the chorus of crickets in nearby foliage, and I looked up with awe at the starry sky. I felt warm in my UDHS jacket, even with a cool nighttime breeze bouncing in small gusts off the creek. Since leaving the building, my mind had been filled with reflections on what I had learned over the years at church and Young Life, that God truly loved me, but I had placed between Him and me the sins of disobedience, pride, selfishness and self-reliance. There is a Scripture which says, in part, "*Your iniquities have separated you from your God*" (Isaiah 59:2), and although I knew the gulf between God and sinners had been bridged by the redemptive sacrifice of Christ, I had never really understood in my heart this powerful truth. After a few minutes, I started talking with God, realizing how much I needed Him. I asked Christ to be my Lord and Savior, believing He had paid for my sins of disobedience. I accepted His gift of forgiveness, and invited Him into my life, asking Him for wisdom in the decisions I needed to make about my future.

That night by the creek was a turning point in my youth. I went home and told my parents about my new commitment to a personal relationship with Christ. I even sent a letter to my old girlfriend, apologizing for anything I had done wrong, and I continued praying for direction on what to do next.

During that time, our country was fighting a war in Vietnam, and those jungles were full of blood, dope, and confusion. Back home in America, the Vietnam issue and youth rebellion were turning society upside down, especially in politics and on college campuses. Martin Luther King, Jr., a symbol of peace, was murdered in April. Robert Kennedy, a symbol of hope, was gunned down in June. Large scale riots had broken out in major U.S. and European cities, and the drug culture of the hippie movement was in full swing. Each night on the six-o-clock news, televisions brought the carnage of Vietnam right into the living rooms of families who in their deepest hearts only wanted a safer world for their children to grow up in.

That was the state of affairs in the months surrounding my eighteenth birthday. I knew a college tuition would give me exemption from Vietnam, but my options for college had narrowed after flunking German III. That disqualified me from Yale or Princeton, both of which had expressed interest in offering a sports scholarship. So, with those and other issues facing me, I had some decisions to make, but with my new understanding and awareness of Christ, I felt a fresh confidence going forward.

During the summer after graduation, I worked as a lifeguard at a private swimming pool. I also attended Young Life events, while working hard to get in top shape physically. Choosing the right college ended up being a pretty easy decision. Even though Penn State recruited me, I opted for the University of Massachusetts because Ken Barr's uncle, Homer, was the head wrestling coach, and he offered me a scholarship. In September of 1968, I began my freshman year. Homer Barr, a three-time heavyweight All American, took an interest in me from the start. At times, Coach Barr was hard on me, one time pinning me repeatedly just to show how much I needed to learn, and how much I could learn from him.

When I started at UMass, I knew I needed some Christian friends. I met the local leaders of InterVarsity Christian Fellowship and Campus Crusade for Christ® (Cru®), but I was not willing to let myself really be discipled. With all the liberties of not living at home, and the college campuses radically changing with student rebellion and confused ideas about freedom and morality, I let down my guard and really messed up in my freshman year. I liked going to the parties, meeting girls, hanging out, staying up late and not showing up for class in the morning. It was all a lot of fun, but my spiritual life was faltering, and at the end of the semester I barely scored a high enough GPA to qualify for coming back the next semester.

During the second semester, I attended class even less, and I went into an academic tailspin. When the final exams were graded, I flunked out of school. This was embarrassing, how I had taken so much opportunity and not made good on it. Back at home, my parents cried with me as I broke the news to them.

The following semester I lived at home, got a job delivering flowers for a florist, and went to a community college two nights a week for the twelve credits needed for getting back into UMass. During that time, Young Life and Ken Barr came more into the picture, and I started growing in my spiritual walk.

In January of 1970, academically and spiritually I was back in shape. I returned to UMass and continued my involvement with Young Life. One time, the well-known Christian public speaker and author, Josh McDowell, was invited to our college, and also to do an evangelistic talk at the local high school where we had started a Young Life program. We rode in the car with Josh, where we prayed with him, and then at the high school we watched him deliver a dynamic message. Being around strong Christian leaders gave me a taste of the wisdom which says, *"The one who walks with the wise will become wise, but a companion of fools will suffer harm"* (Proverbs 13:20).

In 1971, while maintaining decent grades, I won the conference title as a heavyweight, and the following year I repeated as conference champion. A highlight was when our team beat Springfield College, which had been the powerhouse for all of New England. I had gone to UMass because of Coach Barr, who taught me if I train with a heavyweight who is better than me, I will get better. "You migrate to the level of your competition," he said. Homer was a far more experienced wrestler, and every time we got out on the mat, he beat the tar out of me. We trained every day, and he would just work me, over and over. The Bible says that, *"Iron sharpens iron, and one man sharpens another"* (Proverbs 27:17). Ken and Homer Barr, along with a wrestler/coach named John Peterson whom I would soon meet, were that iron in my life, in both physical and spiritual training.

The next year, at the 1973 NCAA finals, I finished in the top 12, and the following year, my last year of wrestling in college, I dropped a weight class, down to 190. My reason for doing this was the heavyweight class was dominated by a 440-pound defending national champion named Chris Taylor. No heavyweight in the country wanted to face Chris, including me, which meant each week I had to starve myself down to 190 pounds in time for weigh-ins shortly before the meet.

Wrestling at 190 was difficult, and I got beat in the New England championship tourney, which meant I did not go to the nationals. Coming out of college, I did not expect my career choice was going to be competitive wrestling.

I look back at my college experience as a roller coaster. A lot of the ups and downs were from choices I made, the people I hung out with and allowed to influence me, but many times it was just a lack of discipline on my part. On the positive side, during those six years I was involved, on and off, with really good organizations like The Navigators®, Young Life, InterVarsity, Campus Crusade and other Christian groups and churches. I was also one of the original members of the College Church in Northampton. All of those different organizations, and my interactions with them, helped to prepare me for what God had planned.

My experience in college began to show me how sports not only develops character, but also *reveals* it. Athletes, coaches and spectators all see character revealed in sport, such as in how a competitor observes the rules or responds to a call by a referee, or to winning and losing. In the heat of competition, emotions rise, and personalities become magnified. There were times when I competed against a guy and came away with respect for how hard he had trained and how focused he was on the sport. This type of experience in training and competition can result in friendships, trust, and opportunities to share my faith.

During my final years at UMass, I studied what I believed would be useful in the years ahead, including several courses which would develop my understanding of Christian Community. I was looking into the possibility of being a teacher and a coach, until one day I received a letter from Cru's sports ministry, *Athletes in Action* (AIA).

UMass Wrestling Team, 1968-69. Carl in back row,
center-right; Coach Barr on far right

CHAPTER TWO

Athletes in Action

"He who walks with wise men will be wise."
(PROVERBS 13:20, NASB)

T he letter was from Rich Pollock, whom my brother Bob had met at a missionary gathering where my name came up as a prospect for the heavyweight position at AIA. In Rich's letter, and in a subsequent call, he gave a summary of AIA's ministry and history, how a small group of sportsmen followed through on the vision of building teams of accomplished Christian athletes, traveling the country and using sports as a platform for sharing the Gospel. Starting in the late 1960s, a team of about a dozen wrestlers, each one needing to raise his own financial support, started going on tours for weeks at a time, taking their families with them, sleeping in motels or as overnight guests in private homes. They began training and competing with college teams, whose coaches welcomed the opportunity for their athletes to get experience with championship level wrestlers.

Rich explained how AIA developed into East and West teams, each one building a nationwide reputation, drawing large crowds and stirring community interest in local teams. All the while, they used the exhibitions as opportunities for sharing the Gospel in a deeply personal way. Imagine a rock-solid athlete, tough as nails, and after earning the crowd's respect through athletic performance, then using the crowd's attention to share a personal testimony about salvation in Christ and the joy of living for Him. Also, over time, they developed a full program of entertainment, involving crowd-pleasing athletic exhibitions of strength, quickness and agility, demonstrating the U.S. and Olympic styles of amateur wrestling, and also a comedy skit that mimicked professional stunt-wrestling. Rich told me, in so many words, "We travel, we train hard, and we use competition, clinics, and sports-entertainment as a way of getting opportunities to share the message of Christ in a personal way." The idea of joining sports and ministry got my attention, and when Rich said to me, invitingly, "We need a heavyweight." I agreed to meet the team at a weekend gathering near State College, Pennsylvania.

In November of 1974 I drove down from Massachusetts to spend a couple days with the guys. I had long hair, a mustache, and very quickly after finishing my college wrestling career I had grown a big belly. There were fifteen wrestlers on the team, including John Peterson, a silver medalist from the 1972 Munich Olympics, who also served the team as the coach. Another wrestler was Reid Lamphere, who also served as the team director and had his sights set on the 1976 Olympics. I quickly saw these athletes with AIA were no slouches when it came to training and competition, but most importantly for me, they valued the spiritual even more than the physical. Some of those guys had sacrificed promising careers in other fields, such as business or teaching and coaching, to offer their lives to Christ in a traveling ministry, needing to raise their own financial support! When I realized all of this, I knew it was something I wanted in my own life. Those men were strong believers as well as elite athletes, and after struggling in my walk with Christ through my college years, I knew I needed the discipline and accountability they offered.

During that weekend, one of our workout assignments was to run up the side of a mountain, do exercises on the top, and then turn around and run back down. At the coach's word, we all took off, and it did not take long for me to be way in the back. After a while, it was all I could do just to put one leg in front of another while pulling in whatever air my lungs could still find a place for. I watched the guys getting further and further ahead, and I just kept telling myself, "Run, run, run." Finally, I stopped to lean over with my hands on my knees, pulling in air for maybe half a minute before standing up straight and pushing further up the hill. After the third time of stopping, while I leaned over and gasped for air, with both hands on my knees and my eyes stretched wide while staring at the ground, all of a sudden I noticed the other guys passing me by on their way back down! After the last one had passed, I turned around and followed them to the bottom, grateful for how much easier it was to run downhill than up.

At that time, probably nobody in the camp believed I could make it at their level of discipline and competition, and I knew I had my work cut out for me. I caught the edge of some jokes, such as "that hippy from UMass won't last more than a few months," but as the weekend continued, and they saw the effort I was putting in, they invited me to an upcoming tournament in East Stroudsburg, Pennsylvania.

I went to the tournament, sometime near the end of the year, and I ended up losing in the semi-finals in overtime. In the consolation finals, I lost again in overtime. It was clear to me and to everyone else I had the skills and training to compete at their level, but after the tournament, a friend named Walter said to me, "There is one more move you have to learn. The three-mile run."

Endurance.

After that tournament, the coach invited me to be a part of the team. Although it could not become official until I went through six weeks of staff training at Colorado State University in Fort Collins, I agreed to start training and touring with the team. We were based in Lancaster, in the center of the Amish countryside of Pennsylvania, where I was given a room with the single guys. The coach explained once I was formally a staff member in the organization, I would need to raise my own funding, but until then I would be given $150 a month with a free bed. I told the coach and the team I was all in, and I got busy working on my three-mile run.

My main workout partner was John Peterson, who would usually beat the tar out of me. After a two-hour practice, when most of the team had left, John and I would stay and work for more than a half hour extra. I was weighing 230 and John was 180, so I could stop him for the first five or ten minutes because of my weight, but by the end he would shoot in on me and take me down. Coach Homer Barr had told me, "You migrate to the level of your competition," and I knew those grueling workouts with an Olympic medalist would raise my level in many ways.

John was also a spiritual coach to me, telling me, "Winning a match or a title is a wonderful thing, and an athlete should work hard to do his or her best, but the true victory is the character we show in wrestling for the prize of honoring God." He may not have said it in exactly those words, but that was the wisdom he aimed to instill in me. Before long, I was in the best shape I had ever been in my life, physically and spiritually.

I began touring with the team and won my first 12 matches, including a major upset in the first week of February. In a dual meet, we went up against our biggest rival, the New York Athletic Club (NYAC). We were losing most of the way, but the turnaround started in the next-to-the-last match, when John Peterson pinned his opponent. Now, the outcome depended on the heavyweight match, and I was going up against a star who had finished second in the NCAA championships. With about 2,000 spectators packed into the gym, and almost every one of them expecting the NYAC star to destroy the unknown Carl Dambman, I stepped onto the mat and gave it my all.

Throughout the match, my opponent kept racking up points and stretching the lead. With less than thirty seconds remaining, he made a mistake, and I was able to pin him. My grueling workouts with John Peterson really paid off, and AIA's organizational news release for that date said:

> "AIA's East Wrestling Team continues to power its way through 1975, remaining undefeated in dual meet competition, including a…victory over the New York Athletic Club…The victory for AIA came on two pins by the final wrestlers, player/coach John Peterson at 190 and rookie heavyweight, Carl Dambman. In the final match, Dambman was down by seven points before pinning his opponent with 14 seconds remaining."

After that victory, we did not have a lot of time to celebrate, since we needed to be back in Lancaster and up early the next morning to head out for a two-week tour. Traveling with the team, and with Rich Pollock as my discipler, I learned how to share my testimony in three minutes and the Gospel in eight, and also how to use *The Four Spiritual Laws* booklet in one-on-one witnessing.

We trained hard, not only in wrestling, but also in spiritual preparation and in rehearsals for athletic demonstrations and skits to entertain the crowds. One of our fan-pleasing stunts was for me to take somebody from the crowd, pick him up and press him several times over my head, and then tell everyone how my true strength comes from knowing Jesus Christ as Lord and Savior. Another part was a juggling demonstration by Reid Lamphere, who would talk about his Christian faith with the crowd while he juggled two balls and an apple, doing various stunts to illustrate important spiritual points.

All through the stunts and exhibitions, each of us would have opportunity to share a short testimony as the crowd listened, illustrating a principle summarized in the saying, "Focus on the fun part, and they will listen to the evangelistic part."

We also provided entertainment by doing a five-minute satire on pro wrestling. As I stepped onto the mat wearing a robe and a nylon stocking over my head, our narrator would theatrically introduce me as *Baron von Crusher,* "the meanest, nastiest, dirtiest wrestler in the world!" He would say a few other things to build up tension among the crowd as they wondered what this frightening bully was about to do. Then, a small wrestler would walk toward the mat, with the narrator introducing him as *Evil Boweevil.* The smaller athlete would come out looking like the last wrestler in the world who could stand a chance against the mighty Baron. As the crowd leaned forward in their seats, I would throw off my robe and loom over the little guy, who then proceeded to use different tricks until, a couple minutes later, I went down and he pinned me. The crowd would burst into applause for the victorious underdog, while I climbed to my feet with my face twisted up in mock anger, playing to the end the role of a defeated bully.

Carl intimidating the audience by playing the role
of "pro wrestler" Baron von Crusher

After the entertainment, our narrator would say something like, "These guys are all wearing a mask, pretending to be something they are not." He would pause a moment for effect, with the crowd wondering where this story was going, and then, with a more serious tone, he would say, "Isn't that what we all tend to do? Walking through life wearing a mask?" He would give a couple seconds for his words to sink in, and then he would say, "But there is One person who did not wear a mask, and I want to tell you about Him." Tens of thousands of people heard the Gospel shared in this way during our four-month tour through the eastern United States. After each demonstration, the wives of the wrestlers on our team would collect the comment cards we had passed out at the beginning. After leaving the gym or arena, back in our places of lodging, we would read those cards and pray individually over each one.

I began writing monthly prayer letters for mailing out to friends and potential future supporters, trying to get across in just a few words what God was doing through AIA. In my February 1975 letter, I wrote:

> "On January 6th I became a part of the AIA East Wrestling Team...AIA teams compete with major college and university teams throughout the U.S. We also share our faith in Christ with the audience through half-time presentations as well as speaking engagements in high school assemblies, college gatherings, church services, and civic clubs...We have spoken to about 40,000 people in live audiences so far this season... There is such a need for people to hear the Good News presented in a clear and simple fashion...Just this past week over 200 high school students indicated they had asked Christ into their lives as a result of an assembly program we gave near Pittsburgh...Pray that I will dig into His Word each day, that I may be a mirror of His love in both my actions and my words, and that I will work hard in practice in preparation for the national tournaments."

For about four months we did almost non-stop sports ministry from city to city, state to state. We traveled thousands of miles in vans and station wagons, sleeping in cheap motels or in the homes of generous hosts, honing our wrestling skills and building each other up in the strength of teamwork, spiritually and physically. Those months really were a whirlwind of sports and ministry events.

The 1975 AIA Wrestling Team won the National Freestyle Championship

Not everyone appreciated our public sharing about Jesus Christ and how a personal relationship with Him can transform even the most downcast and hurting life. One day a high school principal stopped us right in the middle of our presentation and would not allow us to continue. In one Pennsylvania city, where we had been invited by a wrestler named Doug Klenovich, we were denied access to the public schools. The following are excerpts from local, front page newspaper clippings:

> "The Athletes have been at the center of a recent controversy involving the presentation of their assembly program to students in the Greenville Area School District." -Herald staff writer, Robert B. Swift.

> "The AIA East wrestling team [was] denied access to Greenville's public schools for an assembly...The athletes, however, were in Greenville Area High School Thursday morning speaking to a world culture class at

the invitation of its teacher, David Clelland." -Herald Newspaper, Hal Johnson.

They had blocked us from speaking in the gym or the football field, but God showed us a way into the classroom! How could I have known those experiences of resistance and blockades by "key people" were preparing us for pioneering international sports ministry in countries where openly talking about Christ was not only frowned upon but, in many places, severely punished by civil and religious authorities.

One day at home I told my dad about my need to raise financial support. He walked to his desk where we sat down and pulled out a yellow writing pad on which he wrote the names of people he believed I should contact as potential supporters. Rather than a career of teaching and coaching in schools, I was stepping out in faith for what would become a career of ministry through sports.

Starting with my dad's list, and after much prayer, I got busy. The responses began coming back, and I rejoiced with excitement at the commitments to support through prayer and/or financing. There was a widow named Harriet Leach, one of my Sunday School teachers, who told me she would support with $5 a month. This support from Mrs. Leach was deeply encouraging to me, like the woman in the Bible who glorified God by giving her *two very small copper coins* (Luke 21:2).

In late June I drove to Colorado State University for the two weeks of training I would need to become an official member of AIA, and also for the four weeks of Bible teaching provided by Cru's *Institute of Biblical Studies* (IBS). What an experience, to be surrounded by thousands of mostly young Christians eager to learn and develop as much as God might enable them, all in preparation for going out and sharing their faith more effectively with the world.

The tree-studded rolling hills, hiking trails, freshwater streams and clean, countryside air made for a beautiful environment, and I met a lot of wonderful people. Among the students, a majority of us were single, and the bachelors would jokingly say *IBS* meant "I be single, I be seeking." With several thousand unmarried students on campus, what a great place to meet someone who is like-minded.

Well...

CHAPTER THREE

Noreen

---

*"He who finds a wife finds what is good
and receives favor from the Lord."*
(PROVERBS 18:22)

One of the required classes was Old Testament Survey, where I showed up on the first day a little late and took a seat near the back. After listening to the teacher for a few minutes, I looked over to my left and spotted a really cute blonde. We had only brief eye contact, but those one or two moments stayed with me. After the class, I got up and approached the girl as she rose from her chair, all five-feet-two of her. After introducing myself, she told me her name was Noreen. We struck up a conversation, then went outside and walked to our next class, where we took seats beside each other. I remember hearing in my mind the line of a popular song that said, "Five-feet two, eyes of blue, but oh, what those five feet can do!" After the second class, I asked Noreen if she was interested in going out for an ice-cream cone and maybe a movie. She said, "Sure." That was the start of a romance that would join two life histories into one.

For the next month, Noreen and I built wonderful memories and started forming the special bond God designed for His glory from the beginning. Along with taking our classroom studies seriously, we had great times climbing hills, rafting with friends, going on picnics, and just getting to know each other. I learned she had been born in California and raised near Seattle, where her parents owned 80 acres and her father, a small-church pastor, ran a two-man sawmill. When she described to me the beauty of the land in that area, I looked forward to seeing it and meeting her family. I also learned she had graduated from the University of Washington, with a Bachelor of Science as a Registered Nurse. At that time, she was living in Dallas where she was taking classes taught by students from Dallas Theological Seminary, to help prepare for her dream of being a missionary nurse. All of this was impressive to me. I saw she was truly a woman of God, and I was struck by her physical and her spiritual beauty.

Carl and Noreen rafting on the Poudre River in Colorado

After our time in Fort Collins, Noreen went back to Dallas and I returned to Pennsylvania, where I resumed my place on the AIA wrestling team. Running, lifting weights, and wrestling took up much of the days, with the remainder spent in study, speaking preparation, and staff training workshops. On one tour, in November and December of 1975, we competed and spoke in cities throughout ten different states, and also in Canada. I felt awe and gratitude for the many opportunities to communicate what God had done in my life, and occasionally I would reflect back to that night by the creek, or to some deep conversation I had with one of my mentors in high school or college. The Lord my Shepherd had brought me to places I could not have foreseen, and only He knew where the path would lead in the years and decades to come.

Over the next nine months, Noreen and I sent each other letters and cassette tape recordings. In May of 1976, she took some time off work to visit me in Pennsylvania, where she met my parents and I introduced her to family and teammates as a girlfriend. After Noreen returned to Dallas, I focused mainly on training for the upcoming Olympic tryouts, along with several others on the team who hoped to qualify.

In June, I left Lancaster and headed out toward Ohio for the Olympic Trials, where I qualified to advance to the Training Camp. At the Camp, I qualified as an alternate on the Greco-Roman Wrestling Team. Then, in mid-July, I drove to Montreal as an Olympic Team member.

The time in Montreal was quite an experience. Soviet wrestlers were generally regarded as the best in the world, and it was great to see them compete. I had invited Noreen, but she was not able to get the time off of work. My parents were there, and it was nice to spend time with them, and for all of us to see so many events.

The environment in Montreal was upbeat. Although I did not compete, I met a lot of athletes from the Soviet Bloc. I had always been told the people in those countries were our enemies, but my experience in Montreal was an eye-opener. Those young athletes were our competitors, but they were not our enemies. They had hopes and dreams just like us. They had moms and dads, brothers and sisters, feelings and ideas. They were people, who happened to have been born and raised in countries with different political systems, but who deep down were no different than us.

In addition to seeing some great sports competition, the highlight was being at all of the wrestling matches and seeing my training partner and coach, John Peterson, win the gold medal. John is a serious Christian who is not shy about His faith. In a later interview with Sports Illustrated, published in their February 7, 1977 issue, John testified to the world:

> "Without my athletic ability, I would not be able to serve God in the capacity I now do." That SI article also said, "Athletes in Action preaches the gospel at halftime, but during games they give opponents a devil of a time...All of the AIA wrestlers, ready and willing to discuss their faith with other wrestlers and individual spectators, have committed themselves to a mission for spreading the word of God, and utilize their athletic talent as a means to carry out that mission...Team members make no monetary profit for their athletic ability, rather they see themselves as servants of God fulfilling a mission He has laid down for them...The driving force behind the AIA wrestlers, they explained, is God's love rather than a desire to fight."

Carl at the wrestling arena for the 1976 Montreal Olympics

John Peterson receiving his gold medal in Montreal

After the Olympics, I made a long drive to Colorado for the two weeks of staff training in Fort Collins. The plan was to enjoy some fellowship and hard spiritual work, and then drive to Dallas for some much-awaited time with Noreen. As I drove through Colorado, I began hearing on the radio about a flood in the Big Thompson Canyon, which I knew was very close to Fort Collins where Cru was doing its training. The updates kept coming across the airwaves, and then came the announcement there had been deaths in the flooding. When I reached the campus, I was told at once seven of the staff members from the women's leadership team had drowned up in the hills.

This was a difficult way to start our time together. Emotionally, people were struggling with the question of "How could this happen?" We prayed for those who had lost loved ones, and for those who had survived. There were also dozens of others who died in those floods, and for a day or two, we did not know who was alive and who had died. The Cru leadership played a strong role in helping us all come together and draw on Christ through each other.

The mission of Cru is to partner with churches and other organizations to spread the Gospel worldwide. At the 1976 gathering, one day in the giant Moby Gym, about 4,000 of us were handed a blank map of the world. Dr. Bill Bright, whose wife, Vonette, had barely escaped drowning in the recent floods, challenged each of us to write our names in the area of a country we would commit to praying for in a special way. I immediately wrote my name in the area of the Soviet Union.

I left Fort Collins with a deeper awareness of how God works in mysteries we often cannot understand. Why were those seven Christian women taken off the earth, when they had come for training in preparation for taking the Gospel to the world? There is a Scripture which says, *"The secret things belong to the Lord our God, but the things revealed belong to us and to our children forever, that we may follow all the words of this law"* (Deuteronomy 29:29). I knew, as a Christian, I did not have to understand everything in order to know my calling, as with every other Christian, was to love others in His name and do my share in taking the Gospel to *"the whole world as a testimony to all nations"* (Matthew 24:14).

I headed down Interstate 25, and the next day I was in Dallas with Noreen. She knew a couple of the women who had died in the flood, and she was hit hard by the news. We talked about that, looking at different Scriptures and sharing our understanding. We also talked about things at her job and her church, and about my experiences in Montreal. Sometimes, when I looked at her, I felt an amazement which cannot really be put into words, the beauty of the mystery of God who *made them male and female*" (Genesis 1:27). I knew there could be no other woman for me, and although I did not yet have a ring, one day I invited her to a nearby park "for a walk." She agreed, and off we went.

We entered the park in early-evening and came to a tree-lined, grassy area. Coming to a bench, we sat and talked for a while. At one point, with a slight summer breeze stirring the leaves and mingling aromas of grass and flowers, I felt like we were in a scene from a romance movie. I knew the moment had come. I turned to Noreen and fixed my eyes on hers, gently squeezing her tiny hand as I said in my best romantic voice, "Noreen, will you marry me?"

With her lovely blue eyes fixed on mine, she said, "No, Carl."

That is not how the script was supposed to go. I had thought I knew what I was doing, and the perfect moment had come. She sat up a little straighter and, looking me dead in the eyes, told me, "I want you to be a spiritual leader, and I want our relationship to be mature in all areas." She paused a moment, and then she added, "Also, I don't know you that well."

From her words and expression, I understood her answer was conditional, and I had some work to do. I am a person who, when I see something I want, I pursue it. Noreen was worth pursuing. I already knew my spiritual walk needed more commitment, more focus, and the Lord was using the godly woman I had fallen in love with to stir my motivation. I respected her even more, and when we parted that night, I had already fixed my heart and mind on Christ with a renewed commitment.

Over the next four months, Noreen and I continued corresponding, then, shortly before Christmas, when she had completed her studies in Dallas, I flew there to help move her stuff to Washington. We packed the car and headed off toward Auburn, staying with friends along the way.

As we drove up Interstate 5 to Washington and came to the area near her family's 80 acres, we rounded a turn and suddenly in the distance stood the snow-capped Mount Rainier. The Bible says *"The peaks of the mountains are His"* (Psalm 95:4, NASB), and along with the grandeur of Rainier, in whatever direction I looked, forests of evergreens covered the rolling hills. I had never been to the Pacific Northwest, and as we turned off an asphalt road leading to the property, I immediately fell in love with it.

We made our way down a gravel road, over a narrow wooden bridge, then up to her parents' four-bedroom, ranch-style house with its backyard swimming pool. Stepping out of the car and pulling in the aroma of cedar, hemlock, fir and pine, I looked out at the acres of trees, blueberry bushes, and fields with grazing cattle, all pointing to the word that says, *"O Lord, how many are Your works!"* (Psalm 104:24, NASB).

Noreen's parents and other family members were welcoming toward me, but they were very protective of her and she did not want me to speak with them at that time about the likelihood of marriage. A few days after Christmas, I flew back to Philadelphia. Then, in early January, Noreen flew to Germany for a visit with her sister, Pauline, whose husband, Charles, pastored an English-speaking church in Heidelberg. After her time there, she stopped to visit in Philadelphia, where she described her experience in Germany, and how unchurched Europe had become under the rise of secular humanism, socialism, and materialism. She said to me, "Wouldn't it be great if we moved to Europe? I could be a nurse, and you could get a job at an international school to teach and coach wrestling. We could have a ministry, because they really need Christians there." She was so excited, but I said to her, "Sweetheart, that really sounds wonderful, but remember that German is the only class I flunked in high school!"

We agreed to put the idea on hold until we had a better sense of where the Lord was leading us. The most urgent decision, of course, concerned our relationship. We had been seeing each other for a while, and I do not think either of us had any doubts, so really the time had come. One night we went to a formal dance with my parents at the Rotary Club, where my dad had a long-term membership. After the dancing and all the good food inside the building, Noreen and I left for a drive, just to be alone. I parked the car outside of my family's home, and we just sat there for a while, talking and enjoying each other's company. Noreen looked so stunning, with her dress and the way her hair was fixed. I had been trying to do a better job as a spiritual leader, and in the way I treated and respected her. I knew the time had come for my second try, so I looked in her eyes and said, "Will you marry me?" She smiled and said, "Yes." Even though I had expected this to be her answer, it was a wonderful experience, hearing her say it.

With the decision made, we still wanted to ask her parents for their blessing. From the little I already knew of them, I expected we might have to work through some resistance. We went inside and called, and their initial response was to advise we wait a while. We respectfully told them we were ready now, and they gave their blessing.

Over the next few months, I toured with the team while Noreen and I put together plans for the wedding and for our life together. Finally, I flew to Washington, and in a small ceremony on May 28, 1977, at a little church in an old mining town called Black Diamond, we were married. About seventy people attended, with my brother Bob as the best man, and Noreen's younger sister, Janeen, the maid of honor. A neighbor from across the street made the wedding cake, and Noreen's grandmother made her veil to go with the white dress she had purchased. I wore a blue suit, the only one I had ever owned, and it later became my preaching suit! Noreen's brothers had decorated the car, with cans tied to the end,

Wedding at Chapel Wood Church
with our parents

and after the reception at her parents' home we drove to Seattle with reservations for two nights in a nice hotel. While driving, I would look over at Noreen and think of how we had made this most important decision as humans, not for a few years, but till death do us part—to love, cherish and obey. It was a wonderful feeling.

CHAPTER FOUR

Mexico, Iran, and Bulgaria

---

*"Go into all the world and preach
the gospel to all creation."*
(MARK 16:15)

After leaving Seattle, we spent part of our honeymoon in Yellowstone National Park, enjoying the magnificent scenery and abundant wildlife. From there we drove to Colorado for the six weeks at IBS and Cru staff training. We arrived a little early and had time for some whitewater rafting and backpacking. One day we hiked almost eight miles into the Rocky Mountains, building great memories and really enjoying our life together. This was my second time in Colorado for IBS, where I was no longer seeking and no longer single!

From Colorado, we drove to Philadelphia and headed into our future, starting with three weeks of raising financial and prayer support, experiencing the excitement of seeing God carry through on His promise to provide (Luke 12:22-31). Meanwhile, I had qualified for the 1977 Pan American wrestling championships in Mexico City. The style of wrestling I would be competing in is called Sambo, which has similarities with Judo. This was a big event in the world of wrestling, and a medal would increase my platform for ministry as we toured, competed, and shared our faith. In early September, along with my teammates and their wives, we made our way to Seal Beach on the southern coastal edge of Orange County, California. I suggested to Noreen we could look at this trip as a "second honeymoon." During our three weeks of training in Seal Beach, we stayed with a Christian family close to the home of AIA wrestler Bob Anderson, who would lead us down to Mexico as coach of the U.S. Sambo team.

We trained hard in Seal Beach, doing three workouts a day, running on the beach, going to Judo practice, and even paddling a surfboard to build arm and shoulder strength. Although I had told Noreen to think of this as another honeymoon, there were times I was so sore I half-jokingly told her, "Don't touch me!"

In late September we flew to Mexico City, where the tournament was held at the Social Center Gymnasium. Hundreds of spectators filled the seats, enjoying the pomp and ceremony leading up to the competitions, with flags from about 15 countries draped along the back wall. Adrenaline runs high in events like that, and in the days and hours leading up to my turn on the mat, I reminded myself my identity does not depend on winning a medal. The Scripture says, "*Whatever you do, work at it with all your heart, as working for the Lord, not for human masters*" (Colossians 3:23). I had worked with all my heart, to be sure, and I truly wanted both my training and performance to be an offering to God rather than man. That spiritual knowledge was very helpful, but I would be lying if I said my stomach was not jumping with butterflies.

After the lighter-weight competitions, the heavyweights stepped in. I was wrestling well, and the final match for the gold came down to me and a 380-pound Canadian. Try to imagine stepping onto the mat against a man that size. The biggest battle is really not the physical, but the mental. I looked at his size and told myself, "Be cautious. Endurance and technique will win." When the final buzzer sounded, the ref raised my hand in victory.

At the awards ceremony, I stood on a podium while the cameras flashed on my sweat-drenched body and the U.S. national anthem filled the arena. I felt the thrill of victory as my teammates and hundreds of spectators watched an official place the gold medal around my neck. For the next hour I mingled with teammates and coaches, did some short interviews, and nodded in appreciation at the many words of congratulation. Then, finally getting away from the crowd to change clothes in the musty locker room, as I lifted the ribbon off my shoulders, it snapped. I thought, "Well, that is fixable," and then I held the thin, gold colored medal under a light, and I noticed it had little scratches. My mind went to the words of Scripture, where the apostle Paul wrote:

> *"Do you not know that in a race all the runners run, but only one gets the prize? Run in such a way as to get the prize. Everyone who competes in the games goes into strict training. They do it to get a crown that will not last, but we do it to get a crown that will last forever." (1 Corinthians 9:24-25)*

After much training, sacrifice, and discipline, I had won a prize which already had scratches and a broken ribbon. I knew in a few years, hardly anybody would even remember who won the Pan American tournament in 1977. My result on that day was a perishable prize and the applause of people who would soon go on to other things, and what would this all mean after the test of time? It was great to have won the fading little medal, but far greater is the prize of having wrestled through life for God's glory, to receive from Christ the prize of hearing Him say, *"Well done!"* (Matthew 25:23).

After Mexico City, we went to a Pacific coastal town named Mazatlán. We stayed for three days with two AIA teammates and their wives, each couple paying only $8 a night for rooms in a motel near the beach. One day on a small boat I hooked a ten-foot-long sailfish, which I thoroughly enjoyed wrestling out of the ocean and into the boat. So, after winning the Pan Am championship, the Lord added the blessing of a second honeymoon for my wife, along with a good fishing story!

Carl receiving the gold medal at the Pan American
Wrestling Heavyweight awards ceremony

AIA Teammate Bob Walker and Carl land
sailfish off the coast of Mexico

After returning to Pennsylvania, I got busy gearing up with our team for the next tour. Earlier in the year, I had been asked to take on new responsibilities with AIA. Our team director, Reid Lamphere, summarized it in a letter of appreciation to my supporters:

> "As director of AIA East Wrestling Team, I wish to extend thanks for your faithful prayer and financial support of Carl Dambman...This year, he will also be assuming the job of program director and be responsible for accepting and assigning all of our speaking engagements...It's going to be a busy year for Carl."

A few weeks before our November tour, I taught for a week alongside two AIA teammates at a wrestling camp in Millersville, Pennsylvania. Nearly a hundred teenage wrestlers, after training with us during the day, listened to us talk about using our love of wrestling as a way of honoring God and drawing closer to Him. Soon after, we drove to Lancaster, where AIA friends helped us find an apartment on West James Street. For the next couple weeks, I did a lot of local speaking, while also setting up arrangements for the upcoming tours.

We kicked off our season by winning a local match against Franklin and Marshall College on November 8th, but the greater win was spiritual, with over sixty people responding to our sharing the Gospel by either praying to receive Christ, or expressing interest in hearing more. On the 10th, we left for our southern tour through several states. After wrestling in Alabama, we spoke in five fraternities and two dorms, and in Tennessee our wives had opportunities to talk with university students in a variety of classes. At each location, after competing, we gave demonstrations, interspersing the activities with three-minute testimonies and ending with an eight-minute Gospel presentation. We did this all over the eastern United States.

At the time, I did not realize how difficult this new situation was for Noreen. It was comfortable for me, because the culture of wrestling was where I had my identity, and I knew my role in the AIA ministry. But Noreen was accustomed to her working identity as a nurse, surrounded by medical staff and focused on the needs of patients. She struggled to understand how she fit in and how she could contribute on a traveling team of missionary wrestlers. That first year was tough for her, and I was not as sensitive to this as I should have been.

Each of us was still in the early stages of learning our primary identity needs to be in Christ, not in what we do, but in who we are in Him. Over time, Noreen and I would grow together in this, and God used our experiences, the ups and the downs, to glue us deeper in the oneness of marriage as He designed it.

One day back in Lancaster, AIA informed Reid, John, and I that we had been chosen as members of a team representing the U.S. at international competitions in Iran and Bulgaria. This would be my first trip overseas, and in my prayer letter for December I wrote excitedly, "I will be in Iran and Bulgaria until Dec 20!" Some wrestlers from the AIA-West team were chosen, including Don Zellmer, with whom I would do a lot of ministry in years to come. Also recruited to join us was a national champion from Oklahoma State named Steve Barrett, who would later join AIA and become one of my closest friends and long-term ministry teammates. At the time, none of us could have foreseen what God was preparing by bringing us all together for that trip.

We would be going up against some of the best wrestlers in the world, as the first all-Christian team to compete in either country. Using sports for ministry was fairly new in church history, and Athletes in Action, having established its athletic credibility and Christian testimony in the USA, was now pushing out on the international stage.

In early December we boarded a plane and headed off to Iran. The Shah was still in power, but time was running out on his perishable throne. The day came, and we walked into an arena with 12,000 spectators, including the Crown Prince, whom we were told would hand out awards at the end. All of the American athletes would be challenged with jet lag and high altitude, which would make the last few minutes of our matches really tough. At that level of competition, even small disadvantages can make a big difference.

In my first match, I beat an East German, but it was a rough win. During the battle I got a bloody nose and a couple chipped teeth. When the ref raised my hand in victory, my opponent walked off the mat with steady strides while I gasped for air and struggled to stay on my feet. Reid, standing nearby and observing the irony, laughingly pointed to me and then to the German, saying, "*Here* is the thrill of victory, and *there* is the agony of defeat!" I guess somebody tried taking a picture, because I heard John Peterson say, "Don't you dare take a picture of Carl looking like that!" As the day went on, John Peterson and Steve Barrett won medals, whereas I lost my next match to a Bulgarian world champ, and then, in my final match, I lost to a Russian giant with metal teeth. Tough losses, but good experience.

After leaving the arena, we got on a bus and I plopped down in one of the few empty seats. I was physically and mentally exhausted, just sitting there smelling the odor of a crowded bus on a hot summer day. All of a sudden, I caught a strong whiff of garlic and unwashed clothing. I looked up and saw a small Iranian wrestler stepping toward me. His dark-skinned and whisker-stubbled face showed a cheerful appearance, and he said to me in English through a thick accent, "I saw you wrestle. You were very good. Let me kiss you." I needed a moment to process what he had just said, and in that moment his face moved in toward mine. If we were in America, I might have done a rapid leg grab and flipped him on his back. I knew this little guy was from a culture where a kiss was a strong show of respect and admiration, and Cru had trained us well in cross-cultural interactions, but I was not about to let that man kiss me on the lips. I quickly lowered my face so he kissed my forehead. Wow, that was a baptism by fire. Amazing, how different one culture can be from another.

While in Tehran, we met with the Middle East Ministry Director, who set up two speaking engagements. One of the opportunities was at an international high school where diplomats, military personnel, and people in the oil industry sent their children. We did a full program for the students, with exhibitions, a wrestling skit, testimonies, and an explanation of the Gospel.

Out on the streets and in the shops of Tehran, the many sports fans treated us like celebrities, but it was quite a different story with the university students. On our last day, a large crowd marched into the cafeteria as we ate, and they were not looking for autographs. One of them grabbed the American flag from our table and threw it to the ground, where they took turns stomping on it. They seemed to know just enough English to tell us how much they hated us and wanted us out of their country. We knew those kids could be dangerous, so we walked outside and headed to our dorms. The crowd followed us the entire way, and after we went inside to our place on the sixth floor, we could see the students through the window as they shouted threats against us. We went into prayer, and we kept praying. Then, the next thing we knew, they were all gone. We thanked God for His intervention.

We left Tehran with gratefulness for the hospitality shown by many, and for the opportunities to represent the U.S. in competition and to share Christ with many, but the rage and hatred of the students disturbed us. None of us knew how bad things would get in that country over the next couple of years, but we knew how desperately they needed the message of God's love through a saving, personal relationship with Jesus Christ.

Wrestling team trophy and medals in the Tehran arena

Wrestlers and coaches gathering before
the match in Sofia, Bulgaria

After leaving Iran, we flew to Vienna where we picked up Bud Hinkson, the Area Director for Eastern Europe and the Soviet Union, along with some boxes of Bibles and literature for the trip to Bulgaria. Bud was a person you just wanted to be around. He was so positive, he knew the Scriptures, and he was a great encourager with a wealth of wisdom. He would later become a major influencer and mentor to me.

During our time in Bulgaria, one of the Christians from a nearby church came to meet with us and shared his testimony. As I listened, it really struck me how those Christians had remained faithful even when their governmental and educational leaders mocked them for their faith. Atheistic communism had created a culture and a doctrine which characterized belief in God as something for fools and cowards and for old people still stuck in superstitions of the past. Along with being looked upon by the wider society as fools, they could also be punished for doing anything Christian outside the four walls of the church. I thought about how different life was for people of faith in communist countries, compared to my experience of growing up as a Christian in Pennsylvania. As I listened to that testimony, I felt a tug on my heart.

After wrestling and sharing our faith covertly in Bulgaria, we left the communist world and spent a day in Vienna. We were feeling good about all God had walked us through as a team, and we looked forward to getting home to our wives and families. Bud Hinkson accompanied us on the bus ride to the airport, and at one point he rose from his seat to address us. We all stopped whatever we were doing and gave our attention to Bud. After a moment of silence, he said, "I want you guys to move to Vienna. I want you to use wrestling to open doors for ministry all through Eastern Europe."

It took a second for Bud's words to sink in. I thought of Noreen's excitement after coming back from Europe a year earlier, bubbling with passion for moving there and doing ministry in what had been described as a spiritual graveyard. Now, a year later, having seen for myself just a glimpse of it, I knew the time had come for us to seriously and prayerfully consider if the Lord was leading us to make such a move.

At the airport, we boarded the plane and started our long flight across Western Europe and the Atlantic. When I got home, after the normal hugs and greetings, I said to Noreen, "Sweetheart, Bud Hinkson

wants us to move to Vienna and do ministry behind the Iron Curtain."
She stared at me for a second, her eyes bulging with amazement, like she
could hardly believe what she had just heard. What a joy, to have a wife
who really loves the Lord, and who wants her lifetime to count forever
by offering it to God in fulfilling our part of the Great Commission
(Matthew 28:18-20). We both felt drawn by the invitation to Vienna,
but we had our commitments with AIA-East, so it would not be an easy
decision.

Carl and John with their gold medals from Mexico and Montreal

CHAPTER FIVE

On the Move

———

*"My sheep listen to My voice, and I know
them, and they follow Me."*

(JOHN 10:27, NASB)

A few days after returning, Noreen and I had our first Christmas together, and two weeks later we were back on the road with our team. We spent a week in West Virginia, came home for four days, then left for a month-long tour which started in Canada where we worked with Navigator staff. In Canada we wrestled, entertained, shared the message of Christ, and did follow up with those whom we had shared with a year earlier. I was seeing more and more the value of partnerships and networking in sports ministry.

From Canada we went to Whitewater, Wisconsin, where we had a match during their worst blizzard in two decades. Some of the 150 students who attended actually skied their way from nearby dorms to the gym! Overall, almost 30 prayed to receive Christ, and 10 others expressed interest in learning more. I do not remember much about the matches that day, but only the joy of sharing our faith with a gym filled with students all snowed in on a freezing winter day.

About that time, we started hearing reports AIA would be merging its two teams and basing the combined team in the west. This made sense strategically, since it would boost the overall level at which AIA could compete, but it would also mean the wrestlers and their families from the east would need to relocate to southern California. That would make our decision for Vienna easier.

In April, at a dual meet with the Soviet team in our home base of Lancaster, before a crowd of more than two thousand, I wrestled the legendary Soslan Andiyev, a three-time world champion and Olympic gold medalist. I was excited about going up against one of the best heavyweights of all time, especially in front of the home crowd! When the day came and I stepped onto the mat, I knew I could not let Soslan's mystique intimidate me. In the center of the mat, we looked each other in the eye as we did the customary handshake, and then the ref blew his whistle. I started off well, scoring the first point! Unfortunately, it would be my only point. Soslan had superior technique and strength, and in the third period he was beating me by a couple of points when I tried to lock him up for a throw. I made my move, but instead of me landing on top, it went the other way.

Although I got pinned in front of the home crowd, that was outweighed by our opportunity to give testimonies and share the Gospel with the audience, as the Soviet wrestlers looked on! We trusted God that our testimonies would break the stronghold of their conditioned idea that faith in God was only for people who are weak.

Soviet team before the match with AIA in Lancaster, PA

Another memorable experience that year was in the national championships against a 400-pounder named Erland Van Lidth De Jeude. Erland's size and rugged appearance had gotten him roles as a villain in movies, including one with Arnold Schwarzenegger. He was

Carl wrestling legendary Soviet heavyweight, Soslan Andiyev

known for pinning his opponents quickly in the first period, but I knew he did not have great conditioning, so my strategy was to gradually tire him out before trying any kind of serious moves for a takedown.

Strategy and endurance gave Carl the victory against 400-pound Erland in New York

In wrestling, there is a small circle within a larger circle. If a wrestler steps outside the large circle, the ref will warn of "passivity." All through the first period, I kept moving away and moving around, but I was warned three times for passivity, which meant I could lose a point if I did it again. The first period ended with no score, and at the start of the second, I was very careful because he was coming off a minute of rest. By the middle of the period, Erland showed signs of getting tired. My strategy was working, and it was time to stop fleeing and start pursuing.

Not long before the period ended, as I moved toward him, he suddenly twisted up his huge, bearded face, then lifted his head and made a loud, gurgling noise. He seemed like he was about to vomit, so I stepped back and saw his coach run onto the mat with a bucket, just in time for Erland to lean over and heave into it. That was not a pretty sight. From that point, I just stood strong, pushing him, moving him. When the period ended, I knew I had the advantage because of my strategy, conditioning, and discipline.

The third period started, and after a minute, Erland was struggling just to stay on his feet. Then, I saw my chance, and I moved in for a single-leg takedown. The big man fell, giving me the win on points. This match became an example I would often use to illustrate principles of spiritual warfare, such as when to flee (from evil), when to pursue (godliness and love), how to fight (the good fight of faith) and to take hold (of the eternal life to which you were called)—1 Timothy 6:11-12.

Soon after the national championships, we were informed that AIA had finalized its decision to combine the teams. To stay with the organization, every wrestler from the Lancaster team would need to move to California OR join the new team being formed by Bud in Vienna! After carefully seeking the Lord's direction in prayer, Noreen and I informed AIA that we wanted to join the team with Bud in Austria.

Reid Lamphere, and his soon-to-be wife, Carolyn, made the same decision, as did Reid's cousin, Tom Lamphere. Also casting in their lots with the Vienna decision was Doug Klenovich, with his wife, Barb, and their two children. There were other teammates who wanted the challenge of pioneering sports ministry behind the Iron Curtain, but their wives were not yet ready.

Each of us has our calling in Christ, with not only the skills for our share of the work, but the right people on our team. My team begins with my wife, as the Scripture says, "'*For this reason a man will leave his father and mother and be united to his wife, and the two will become one flesh.' This is a profound mystery--but I am talking about Christ and the church*" (Ephesians 5:31-32). The Scripture tells us "*we are co-workers in God's service*" (1 Corinthians 3:9), and I believe this co-laboring with God is to be reflected in the co-labor of marriage. My wife works together with me, and in God's arrangement of the parts, I could not have done what I did in life without Noreen at my side.

After we notified AIA's leadership of our decision, they informed us we would need to attend a twelve-week training program in South Central Los Angeles, in a neighborhood called Watts. All the arrangements were made, and in September of 1978 we arrived in Los Angeles. For three months we received intensive training for ministry in cross-cultural situations, along with some basics on how to learn a language. We lived with a black family, and we did outreach in an area with a culture very different than what we had been accustomed to in our own upbringings. Each of us was challenged to go out with a local Christian ministry worker, to share Christ and disciple new Christians. We were also encouraged to begin a Bible study and a prayer group, and to invite local people to a church. During our ministry work on the streets of Watts, we saw 21 people pray and receive Christ. Not everybody appreciated us being there, and I was even accused of being an "undercover cop"! Overall, it was a really wonderful and rewarding time. We met some beautiful Christians, and each of us was used by the Lord to draw others to Him. Also, during that time, the Lord blessed us with the miracle of conception, and we rejoiced in God's gift of a coming new addition to our family.

From Los Angeles, after a visit to Auburn for Christmas with family, we returned to Philadelphia and started packing our bags. Then, on February 18, 1979, a group of family members accompanied us to JFK Airport in New York. At the gate, we all stopped for a final round of hugs and prayers. I saved my best hug for Dad, lifting him completely off the ground and telling him how much I loved and appreciated him. From there, my wife and I turned to face the plane that would take us into our future.

The Bible assures us the world "*is passing away*" and we are to think of ourselves as "*foreigners and strangers on earth*" (1 John 2:17, NASB;

Hebrews 11:13). Why would we leave a comfortable, stable, and predictable life for the risks of the unknown? If I had chosen to rely on my own understanding, I might have done what a brother-in-law would later suggest: "Why don't you just apply for a job as chaplain for the

AIA teammates in California
before moving to Europe

Philadelphia Eagles?" Now, that would have been fun, if I could have gotten such a job, and it would have been safe and predictable. But God had used what Noreen and I glimpsed in Europe to pull on our hearts. The Lord Jesus said, *"My sheep listen to My voice...and they follow Me"* (John 10:27, NASB), and we were thankful God had made so clear to us and to our teammates His leading in this decision. Our guiding wisdom as we left for Europe was the Great Commandment (Mark 12:29-31) and the Great Commission. How could we go wrong with that?

We followed God's call of love toward people in countries where just seeing a Bible was an uncommon experience, and where athletes and coaches had no idea of how God could be an integral part of their lives. We boarded the plane and took our seats. A few minutes later, we felt the push of acceleration, our backs pressing into the cushions, and the world outside our window whizzing by and changing shape until all we could see was sky. As the plane rose in a curve heading northeast, with my wife at my

Carl's family with us at JFK
airport before flight to Europe

side and our baby inside of her, the only thing I knew for certain was we had made the right decision and God would be glorified.

CHAPTER SIX
Vienna

"If I take the wings of the dawn, if I dwell in the remotest part of the sea, even there Your hand will lead me"
(PSALM 139:9-10)

On the following day, we landed in Frankfurt. Noreen's sister, Pauline, with her husband Charles and their boys, welcomed us with joyful faces. From the airport, we went to their apartment in Heidelberg, where Charles handed me the keys to his Volkswagen van and said, "This will help you get started." I stared at the keys, and then at him, struggling to find the words for my amazement and gratitude. Finally, I just said, "Thank you." Charles and Pauline had three children, and on a small-church pastor's salary, trying to make ends meet was often a struggle, so we knew this was really a sacrifice on their part. That kind of gift goes a long way, not just in its material value, but in how it shows that God is saying, "Don't worry, I've got this."

After a week in Heidelberg, we picked up Reid, Carolyn and Tom at the Frankfurt airport. The next morning, we loaded the van and headed south. After a full day on the road, we reached Vienna, where a group of missionaries warmly welcomed us. Doug and his family arrived that same week, and we all got busy learning German and whatever else we needed to know about that part of the world.

A few days later, I received a letter from my father, which started off by saying, "I already miss you, but every time I take a breath, I realize how much you love me." As I was wondering what he could mean by that, I kept reading, only to learn I had cracked two of his ribs while hugging him at the airport! He explained that on their drive home, he began having upper-body pains, and they feared it could be a cardiac issue. They sped to the nearest emergency room, where the doctors quickly diagnosed the cause, telling him, "Mister Dambman, somehow you have suffered two cracked ribs." I do not think Dad told the doctors how it happened, but I sure felt terrible for my carelessness in grabbing my aged father like he was an athlete in his prime. I thanked the Lord he was going to be okay.

We quickly found Vienna an interesting city, with many scenic and historic sites. It is also the music and spy capital of Europe, and a major banking and business hub. Noreen and I rented the second floor in the home of an elderly couple, and along with having our own kitchen, four completely furnished rooms and a large backyard garden, we had a balcony with a view of the beautiful Vienna woods.

In parts of the city, the narrow, picturesque cobblestone streets that look so beautiful on postcards were really a challenge to drive on, especially when dodging trams! Some other things we needed to quickly get used to were the limited shopping hours, high prices, counting with the metric system, registering with local police, and, of course, communicating in German. Do not believe anyone who tells you, "Everybody in Europe speaks English!"

Austria is much more noted for skiing than wrestling, but Cru headquarters was there, and we were an hour's drive from the closest Czechoslovakian city, and four hours from Budapest, so the location was great for access to places behind the Iron Curtain. Of course, we could not get across those borders as missionaries, but this is where sports would come in handy.

We were only four wrestlers with our families, lifting our eyes to the east and seeing a vast field of harvest. We had no playbook for how to build a sports ministry in countries which for decades had been saturated with atheistic communism, but we had faith in Him who opens what *no one can shut* (Revelation 3:7). We also had a strong sense of camaraderie among ourselves. We worked out together, worshiped, trained, learned the language and hung out together. We were best friends.

In the first week, we spoke with people at the nearby University about using their facilities for training, and they agreed to give us access. We also spoke with some members of the Austrian Olympic Committee, and when they realized we had Olympic wrestlers on our team, they offered the use of their great facilities. Meanwhile, we all began attending an English-speaking church where nearly half the congregation was doing undercover missionary work in Eastern Europe. Many of them were skilled laborers who could have earned much larger paychecks in western nations, but who were using their time and skills for access to people in communist countries for the Gospel.

Within a few weeks, we had settled in enough to begin utilizing Europe-wide wrestling competition for ministry purposes. Our first adventure was to Italy for a couple of international tournaments, where Reid and I would compete in both, but Tom and Doug would wrestle in the first and then return to Vienna. Meanwhile, with Carolyn accompanying us on the drive, Noreen would stay back with Barb and her two kids until Tom and Doug returned. After that, Noreen would catch a train to Rome on a ticket she had already purchased. That was our plan.

Doug, Tom, Carl and Reid in Italy with the team trophy

The day came, and we drove to Livorno where three of us won medals. We also developed positive relationships with several of the wrestlers, who took us on a tour to see the Leaning Tower of Pisa. The following day, Tom and Doug boarded the train back to Vienna. That same evening, a Sunday, Noreen left the apartment and walked a mile or so to a place where she could board a trolley. A friend had told her, "Just get on the D-Tram, and it will take you straight to the train station."

Noreen got there early and stopped by a sign with a D that had a slash in front of it. She began her wait, surrounded by the sounds of people chattering away in a language she could barely speak. After twenty minutes she started feeling concerned, so she turned to a nearby group and said, "Why isn't the D-Tram coming?" "Oh," one of them said in German, "you see the slash in front of the D? That means the D-Tram does not run on Sundays." Noreen could hardly believe what she had just heard. Her train for Rome would be departing, and she had no way of getting word to us that she would not be showing up.

The Scripture says, "*Call upon Me in the day of trouble*" (Psalm 50:15, NASB), and Noreen did exactly that. While she was praying, a woman speaking perfect English stepped toward her and said, "You seem like you need help. Let me help you." Noreen, grateful that she could communicate in her native language, explained the situation. The woman smiled and said, "I am going there too! Just follow me." Noreen followed the woman onto a different tram, but when they needed to change trams, she looked at the schedule and said, "This tram will not get us to the station in time for the train!" The woman said with a bright smile, "I am going there too. Let's just take a taxi!"

Less than a minute later, the woman had hailed down a taxi, and she and Noreen were whizzing through the busy streets of Vienna, arriving at the station in time for Noreen to board her train. She never saw that woman again, and when she got to Rome we could hardly get in a word as she told us excitedly about this "angel" whom God had sent at the trolley line in Vienna.

What an experience that had been for Noreen, and then for all of us when she told us about it. It was just one of those incidents that remind us of how God is in control, even when it might seem like He is not.

In May, our team drove to the U.S. Army base near Heidelberg, where Reid and I met with the head of chaplaincy and the director of sports for Europe. We explained our history of using wrestling events and demonstrations as a platform for testimony and for teaching life skills. At first, they seemed a bit hesitant, until they realized two of us were Olympians and we were part of Campus Crusade for Christ. The meeting ended with both of them agreeing to work with us in providing evangelistic sports demonstrations in a number of military locations later in the summer.

From Germany, we returned to Vienna, and a couple days later Reid and I flew to Romania where the European Wrestling Championships were held. We did not go there to compete, but to meet and develop relationships with coaches and athletes from various countries in Eastern Europe. The Lord blessed our time there, with coaches and officials from more than a half-dozen countries inviting us back for training and competition with their national teams.

Elite athletes in some of those countries were larger-than-life heroes, favored by the governments for boosting national pride with impressive performances in international competition. The top coaching jobs in each sport were political appointments, and the government leaders expected the coaches to train their athletes to be the best. So, when the coaches learned we had championship-level wrestlers, and when we offered to come back and train with their teams, they were eager to set up dates for us. This was our ticket into the forbidden lands behind the Iron Curtain.

Working together with Bud Hinkson in Vienna and AIA headquarters in Colorado Springs, we started setting up tours for training and competition with national wrestling teams in countries like Poland, Hungary,

Reid and Carl in Bucharest for the European Wrestling Championships

and Czechoslovakia. During the competitions, our team of four did well, earning respect from athletes, coaches and spectators, not just by our skills on the mat but also by our sportsmanship. Many of the people in communist countries were conditioned to see Americans as the enemy, but we showed through our conduct and demeanor that we saw them as competitors who had worked hard and deserved our respect.

A typical day involved grueling hours on the mats with the wrestlers, who were then willing to sit for a while and listen to us talk. One by one, we spoke to them in short testimonies and teachings on spiritual things. We explained how God created everything to show His glory and goodness, and "God has given you athletic talent to be used as a way of honoring Him." We had their full attention as we urged them to "give it your all in training and competition, but remember that winning or losing a match does not define who you are."

All of this was new for them. They had been conditioned to believe "winning is everything," and a loss in competition was a betrayal of their nation and failure as a person. I told them about my experience of winning a scratched-up gold medal in the Pan American wrestling tournament, and how my status as champion only lasted until the next winner came along. I said, "We want to tell you about a prize that never perishes, and how you can have a status as champions in the struggle to live for the glory of God who created you."

Their facial responses, with their comments and questions, showed the Holy Spirit was using our witness to change the shape of their thinking. I would often finish my part by saying something like, "Work hard to do your best, but even if the results are not what you were hoping for, you can focus on making your performance an offering to God who loves you." What an incredible experience for us to hear some of those young men asking how they too could have a relationship with Jesus Christ, and to then bow their heads in prayer and receive Him as Savior and Lord.

The coaches in the communist countries quickly realized we were doing more than just wrestling, but they "looked the other way" as we met with their guys after training and explained the value of a spiritual foundation. Many of those young athletes had never heard someone share about Christ and the meaning of salvation in a truly personal way, and their hunger was stirred. We had earned their respect through sports, and by building trust and relationships, they saw how we cared for them as persons and not just as athletes.

In Czechoslovakia, we were training in a sports facility with freestyle wrestlers who had a national coach named Mickey. By that time, my German was far from fluent, but I had the basics and could communicate enough to get by. Well, one day after workouts, Mickey invited me to his hotel room "for a talk." I nodded, then followed him up the steps and through the doorway into his small lodging. After he closed the door behind us, I watched him moving quickly around the room, first pulling down the shades, then grabbing a pillow and setting it over the phone, and finally reaching his hand to an old transistor radio and turning up the music to an awkwardly high volume. After doing all of this, with me standing on a rickety wooden floor in the middle of the room, he stepped closer, glancing toward the door like at any moment it might come crashing in. Then, he set his eyes on mine and, pointing a finger toward his chest, he said, "I am a radish."

I watched him in silence, feeling the closeness of the walls in the tiny room and smelling the staleness of old furniture and sparse ventilation. I started to move my lips, thinking how I could form in German the question, "What in the world are you talking about?" Before I could make a sound, Mickey started explaining he would lose his job and possibly much more if he did not play the role of supporting communist policy and philosophy. "I am red on the outside," he said, "but not on the inside." Now I understood him very well, and I felt for him. In the United States, we grow up with the constitutional rights of freedom of expression and peaceful dissent, but there I was, in a small room on the other side of the world, talking with a man who feared major consequences if the wrong person heard him say anything inconsistent with communist dogma and its atheistic commitments.

I blinked my eyes and nodded, showing with my facial expression that I appreciated what he was telling me, and that he could trust me to be very careful with what I knew. Mickey told me he treasured the freedoms outside the communist world, and the spiritual foundation we were teaching his athletes was needed. "I believe in what you guys are doing," he said, "but I cannot openly express that." Hearing those words from the head coach in a communist nation was amazing and encouraging. After our brief conversation, Mickey turned off the radio, pulled his pillow off the phone, walked to the window and opened the shade, then escorted me to the door where I stepped out in the open air and gave thanks to God for my part in His Great Commission.

With Steve Barret (front row on far right) and the Czechoslovakian team

AIA wrestlers training with the Czechoslovakian team

CHAPTER SEVEN

If Only I Could Remember My Keys!

"And let us run with perseverance the race marked out for us, fixing our eyes on Jesus"
(HEBREWS 12:1-2).

Near the end of June, we traveled to Austria and Poland for Greco-Roman wrestling tournaments where twenty countries were represented. One of my Polish opponents was 6'6" tall and weighed 380 pounds! After the match, while getting three stitches above my eye in a local hospital, I was able to share with the doctor who spoke English well. I learned much about the people, the country, the government, and even a few Polish jokes about Americans! The doctor opened up to spiritual things as I shared my faith and encouraged him to place his trust in Christ.

Also in June, Noreen and I completed a three-month course in German at the Goethe Institute. We still had a long way to go, and those three months were only the first of a three-part series, but we were getting it! German is a common second-language in other countries in that part of the world, and we knew the hard work of learning it would be invaluable for ministry.

Noreen next to me at German language class in Vienna

In July, when Noreen was eight months pregnant, she and Carolyn accompanied the team to Poland on an invitation to provide demonstrations and testimony at youth camps. We drove into the mountains until the roads turned into trails, then we got out and started hiking to the different campgrounds where students stayed for a week at a time. In camp after camp, they cheered at our demonstrations and listened to our testimonies, showing once again the principle that if you provide the fun part, they will listen to the evangelistic part.

In one of the camps, we did our demonstration on a hill in a cow pasture. Using our sleeping bags for mats, we performed with cows in the background and more than 60 students cheering for us. On that trip, we trained with the national team and did demonstrations for good-sized crowds in a chapel, a pasture, a barnyard, an orchard, and a soccer field. We had come a long way from the cushy gyms and arenas of the eastern USA!

First trip to Poland. Wrestling demonstration in
a field with cows in the background

Thankful for good translators and opportunities to share the Gospel

In late-July, with Noreen close to delivery, our baby was breech. We wanted a natural birth, not a C-Section, so we had lots of people praying. Then, during the last week, the baby turned, and God was glorified through the prayers of many.

On the night of August 4th, Noreen was ready. I drove her to the hospital where the doctor admitted her and said to me, "Your wife will not give birth for at least another twelve hours, so you can go home." I left and got home at a late hour, which should have been no problem, except when I searched through my pockets for the keys, I realized I had locked them in the car with our extra set in the house. It was nearly midnight, and I did not want to wake up the owners, so I walked to a pay phone at the end of a trolley line a half mile away. I called Doug and said, "You're not going to believe this, but Noreen is in the hospital and I am locked out of the house." He told me, "Just get on the trolley and come stay with us for the night." I sheepishly thanked him, then took the trolley to their home where I slept overnight on a couch.

The next morning, after taking the trolley home, I found the gate and the front door had not been locked. If I had just thought to check, I could have gotten in! After a quick breakfast, I headed off to the hospital, and a couple hours later our wonderful daughter Elisabeth Anne joined us on this journey at seven pounds and thirteen ounces. Through God's blessing on our work in Europe we had seen many new births spiritually, and now He had blessed us to hold in our arms the amazing gift of a child. When Noreen came home from the hospital, her mom, Norma, had flown in from Seattle. This was Norma's first trip outside the United States, and she had no easy task of learning the process for getting a passport and traveling alone across the world. She was determined to be there and help Noreen. What a beautiful experience of watching Elisabeth in her Grandmother's arms while my wife was getting some much needed rest. Just another one of those memories that tugs at the heart.

Noreen's mom holding Elisabeth in our Vienna apartment

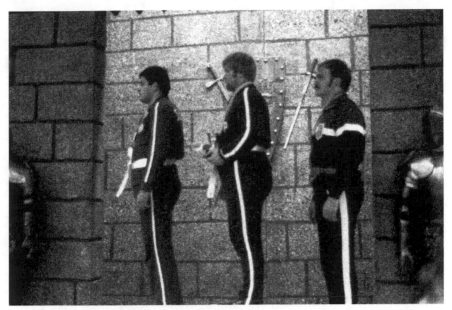

Carl (far right) receiving bronze medal in Madrid,
along with Soviet and Bulgarian wrestlers

In October, Doug and I flew to Madrid for the Sambo Wrestling World Championships. I won a bronze and had the opportunity to share the Gospel with an Israeli wrestling coach named Alex, who was an English-speaking Russian Jew and an agnostic. Alex had many questions and showed a lot of interest. We also shared through a translator with many of the Spanish wrestlers, leaving them with literature printed in their language. Spain is a land the apostle Paul probably spent more than a month getting to for the Gospel's sake (Romans 15:28). Although Paul himself was not an athlete, his Spirit-inspired letters are loaded with athletic expressions connecting to spiritual warfare and the furtherance of the Gospel. One of the reasons for my writing this book is to illustrate, with stories of actual people and events, how God has given sports as a wonderful means of evangelism, leadership training, and worship.

In both the west and east, the responses in Europe were exciting. We did programs in February for the chaplains on two military bases near Frankfurt, along with several more in different venues in the area. In Austria, after a program at a college prep school, one of the students wrote in a comment card: "It was one of the best exhibitions I have ever seen. You were not afraid to let it be known that you profess Christianity."

Sadly, we often encountered resistance in the churches to the very idea of using sports in ministry. Many of the old guard saw athletic conditioning and competition as something that leads to pride and a materialistic focus. Through patience, reasoning, and personal testimony, we were able to start changing their way of looking at this. We helped them to recognize sports as a universal language can bridge cultures and communities, leading to respect and friendships that open doors for sharing Christ. Some of the churches were already in agreement that athletics can be a platform for evangelism, but they needed help in understanding how sport itself can be a way of drawing closer to God and honoring Him. The Bible is clear in teaching God created everything to show His glory and goodness, so why should anyone doubt sports is something the Lord intended mankind to use in worshiping Him?

Meanwhile, along with having come to Vienna for missionary work, we were also focused on training for the 1980 Olympics. We wanted to improve as athletes, and Eastern Europe was very strong in wrestling. Training and competing with those guys gave us an edge, so we had the double advantage of wrestling with some of the best in the world, while also bringing the message of a personal relationship with Jesus.

Then, in February of 1980, because of the Soviet troops in Afghanistan, President Carter officially announced a U.S. boycott of the Moscow Olympics. We still clung to the small chance of a diplomatic breakthrough allowing us to compete, although we knew it was only a tiny thread of hope. Try to imagine training for years for the biggest competitive event of your career, and then you are told it is probably not going to happen. News of the boycott made it a lot harder to get up for a vigorous training session at seven in the morning.

Olympics or no Olympics, we still had the greater race to run. One of my favorite verses in sports ministry is Hebrews 12:1, which uses the Greek word *agon*, from which we get our English word *agony*. In that verse, the Scripture tells us to *"run with perseverance the race [agon] marked out for us."* A related word from the same root is used in Luke 22:44, where the Scripture records that Jesus, *"being in anguish [agonia], he prayed more earnestly."* Any 1980 Olympic hopeful who tells you he or she was not in *anguish* over the boycott is either lying or was never serious in the first place. Yes, as Christians we wanted our love for sports to glorify God, and the boycott was not the final word on our identity, but it really did hurt. Still, we saw it as an opportunity to practice what we preach, to run with perseverance the *agon* marked out for us. A week after learning of the boycott, we went to Budapest for international competition and sharing. We went, we wrestled, we witnessed.

One night during the weekend of the tournament, when we had gone to bed thanking God for blessing the work of ministry and thinking of our dear families hundreds of miles away, a sudden knock on the door startled us from our rest. Was this the secret police, coming to toss us out of their country for using wrestling as a cover for sharing Christ? I pulled on my jeans and opened the door. Instead of the secret police, it was a group of wrestlers with eager looks on their faces. Before I could say anything, one of them blurted out, "We want to know more about Jesus Christ!" Wow.

Our bodies were tired from a long day in the gym, but our spirits rose up in excitement at the eagerness of those young athletes to learn about the Lord. Everyone got up, and we all found places to sit. They asked questions, and we walked them through the Four Spiritual Laws booklet. They hung on every word as we spoke from the heart and told them, "As athletes, the world teaches you to be results-oriented, so that your life is up and down, depending on your latest production, your latest results in competition. What a miserable way to live! But if you learn to find your identity in Christ, then your performance is an offering to God who loves you. So, if you lose a match that could have won the tournament for your team, you will feel the hurt of losing, but it does not define who you are. Always do your best in training and competition, because your motivation is to honor Christ who loves you. But whether you win or lose the match, if you gave your best, you can go home knowing you honored Christ and your identity is in Him, not in your athletic results."

How did we know they were really listening? Because they kept us up until four in the morning, and the next night they were back for more! It was tough on us physically, because the days in the gym were long, and we really wanted more sleep, but God gave us strong bodies for the work, and we rejoiced to no end in seeing those young athletes coming alive in the faith of Jesus.

We encountered this same thing consistently, especially in communist countries, how the people were amazed to see athletes believing in Christ and speaking out for Him. They had been told all their lives faith in God was for people who are weak, and most of them assumed this was true. Now, they were seeing championship-level athletes, even Olympians, talking humbly and passionately, not just about "faith in God," but about a living, saving, personal relationship with Jesus Christ.

In early March, our whole team went back to the U.S. for Olympic tryouts and, for those who qualified, the training camps. Even under the cloud of a near-certain boycott, it was an important time for us. In the Olympic Training Camp, we had a Bible study led by John Peterson's brother, Ben, a wrestler who had won the gold in Munich and the silver in Montreal. About twenty wrestlers attended the studies, and the spiritual hunger of those athletes was a real joy for me.

I made the team again as an alternate, losing in my final match to future Olympic champion Jeff Blatnik, whose quickness and technique earned him the top spot on the team. Steve Barrett and Reid also qualified in their weight categories. Soon after the tryouts, John Peterson announced his retirement from competition. He had won the silver in Munich and the gold in Montreal (the opposite of his brother!), along with two medals from World Championships. John told AIA he would continue as a coach, and he and his family would join us in Vienna early in 1981. This would be a huge boost for our team, not just for the athletic training and leadership John brought, but also for the doors it would open in communist countries. It is one thing to be a national champion or have won international competitions, but to be an Olympic gold medalist is the highest rank one can get. What communist coach would not want a team with John Peterson to train with his guys?

Summer passed, and the Olympics went on without us. But we had our own race to run, our own prize to pursue. The harvest fields were ripe, and as the opportunities multiplied, Bud Hinkson made an urgent call to Don Zellmer back in the States. As Don himself would later recount: "I distinctly remember in 1980, having gotten the phone call from Bud in Vienna, saying, 'Can you come over and help us for a few months!'" Only God could have known those "few months" would stretch into 20 years! Four days later, as Don tells it, "I was on a Pan Am flight to Europe with my bike and backpack. [Sometimes] you just go after it, and the rest is history." Next thing we knew, Don was right there with us in Vienna, with John Peterson and Steve Barrett soon to follow.

At home, we were making good progress in our language studies, although we still made many mistakes, like the day Noreen ended up with four pounds of meat instead of one. On another occasion, when Noreen was eight months pregnant and our neighbors, Wolfgang and Hannah, had us over for dinner. On our way out the door I tried saying, "Thank you for the "invitation," and only after they fell over laughing did we learn I had told them, "Thank you for inducing labor."

On the first day of November, Noreen gave birth to our wonderful son, Jonathan David. He came to us on a snowy afternoon, and I was there to welcome all nine pounds and five ounces of him. Definitely a heavyweight!

After the birth, Noreen and David needed to stay in the hospital for several days, so I took a tram to the new apartment we had recently moved into. Wolfgang and Hannah were babysitting Elisabeth while I was at the hospital. As some backstory, Hannah had given birth to their child on the day Elisabeth was born, with she and Noreen sharing a room and building a warm friendship. A year later, as we searched the big city for a good, affordable apartment, we walked into a lobby and the two women spotted each other. Hannah told us she and her husband lived there, and it was a good place. Next thing we knew, God had shown us to the right apartment with trustworthy friends nearby. We were so grateful for His shepherding hand.

So, having left the hospital and come to our apartment door, I was ready to pounce on a pillow, but when I searched my pants' pockets, I could not find the keys. After standing there a minute, shaking my head in disbelief and irritation, I walked back to the trolley line and took a tram to the hospital, telling my resting wife I had locked my keys in the apartment. She gave me her set, and I took a tram back home. Once inside the apartment, after wearily pulling off my sweater, what did I see but the keys sticking out of my shirt pocket! I just laughed and thanked God for the blessing of a second wonderful child and the miracle of birth.

CHAPTER EIGHT
Zakopane

___

*"Do not be afraid; keep on speaking because
I have many people in this city."*
(ACTS 18:9-10)

A few months after David's birth, Noreen's brother Bill and his wife came to visit. Sharing our children and our life in Europe with them was so precious to us, and helped them relate better to our new situation. By this time, Elisabeth had begun to talk more, and David was a very active little boy, crawling around and climbing everywhere. Most of our family was able to visit us over the years. Each visit was such a delight and often an adventure when they traveled with us, especially in eastern Europe. Our family and friends were impressed with how Noreen had become fairly adept, with the help of a double stroller, at getting around shopping and other ventures with our little ones!

In February, John Peterson arrived with his family, and the Barretts came in June. Two huge additions, both physically and spiritually. In July, we all took a trip to southern Yugoslavia, where one night we had four Muslim athletes in our hotel room. We outlined parts of the Old Testament, showing how Islam and Christianity agreed basically about creation and the fall of man. Then, we showed Christianity's answer to the problem of sin—Christ's death on the cross. That was probably the first time those men had heard a clear presentation of the Gospel. They were open to what we had to say, and we told them we would be back in September.

Amazing, how God was using sports to give access and presence we could not have gotten without our gifts and training in athletics. It calls to mind Paul's instruction for Timothy to "*fan into flame the gift of God*" (2 Timothy 1:6), and also God's assurance that we "*have different gifts, according to the grace given to each of us*" (Romans 12:6). God has chosen to distribute abilities and opportunities "*to each one individually just as He wills*" (1 Corinthians 12:11, NASB), but we are responsible for what we do with these. Paul tells Timothy to "*be strong in the grace that is in Christ Jesus*" (2 Timothy 2:1), thereby reminding him not to think of it as his own power or understanding, but rather that which God supplies. We are to pray like it is 100% up to God, and work like it is 100% up to us, knowing that any positive results come from the Holy Spirit because, "*Unless the Lord builds the house, the builders labor in vain*" (Psalm 127:1).

Of course, we had our share of complications, some big and some a bit tedious, like the day we got detained in Poland two times within four hours. The first time was when one of us spotted an old steam locomotive, something we could probably only see in a museum at home. We stopped the car and took a picture. Next thing we knew, the police came and hauled us off to the nearest station, where they said, "Why are you taking pictures of a military object in our country?" One of us said something like, "We did not know it was a military object, and we are very sorry." They ended up taking our film and letting us go. A couple hours later, in a different city, we saw a really long line at a store that said "Bakery." One of us got out of the car to take a picture, and we were quickly approached by some officers who hauled us in again. They wanted to know why we were taking pictures "for propaganda," and I forget what we told them, but they ended up taking our film again and letting us go. After that, we did not take any more pictures in Poland!`

On another occasion, at the Polish border coming out of Czechoslovakia, the guards spotted a large box of multi-vitamins which had been donated for us to give to the Polish wrestling team. They looked at the vitamins and said, "We have a possible problem here. It looks like you are smuggling drugs into our country." They brought out a little dog to sniff through our stuff, but the only thing the dog showed interest in was my gym bag. One of the guards looked at me and said, "Open the bag." I stooped down, unzipped it, then reached in and set my smelly old wrestling shoes on the ground next to the bag. The dog ran in circles around the shoes, jumping and barking at them. It was like a scene from the Keystone Cops, and we tried to hold back our laughter but just could not do it. The guards seemed embarrassed at how their highly trained dog was zeroing in on my shoes instead of the pills, but they still took the box to a nearby laboratory and made us wait five hours for the results. Such is the life of a missionary.

The summer of 1981 was a busy one. From the beginning of July until the middle of September, we were on the road for 50 out of 65 days. Our trips included tournaments in Austria and East Germany, training in Poland, and the World Wrestling Championships in Norway (Greco-Roman) and Yugoslavia (Freestyle). We did our evangelistic wrestling program in seven different towns in Austria, with hundreds of people hearing the Gospel. From there, we went to Czechoslovakia, where we participated in a training camp and continued building relationships we had already established. Our goals continued to center around winning athletes to Christ, building them in their faith, and sending them out to win others in their country. That has always been our ministry philosophy: Win, build, send.

On the evening of December 12, 1981, for the third time that year, we crossed the border from Czechoslovakia into Poland. Reid did the driving, with John and I packed into his sedan along with Carolyn, who was five months pregnant. Steve and Cindi, with their young daughters, had gone ahead of us a week earlier in their VW Bug. Reid drove until we came to the Sport Hotel in Zakopane, a beautiful mountain resort where the Polish national team often trained. We had scheduled with them for training and had arranged for a Christian translator. The national coach, Eugene, knew we were Christians, and before we had talked with any of the wrestlers, he called us aside and said, "I can teach my athletes the physical techniques, but I can't teach them the spiritual. I need you guys to do that." He told us when we were with the wrestlers away from the gym, he would be gone much of the time, so his guys would feel free to ask and say what they wanted. To hear this from yet another communist-country coach amazed us, and we thanked God for the open door.

At breakfast the next morning, as we talked about our plans for the day, the hotel's public address system suddenly blasted an announcement that went something like, "Attention everyone! Let it be known that at midnight the Polish government declared martial law. You have permission to travel until tomorrow, after which all out-of-city movement will be restricted and only permitted by the decision of the military." For a few seconds, we all sat there and stared at each other. Then, someone pointed out if we had arrived 6 hours later than we did, we could not have gotten into the country. "God has us here for a reason!" somebody said, and after that we all grouped together for prayer.

After a time of giving thanks to God and asking for safety and guidance, we went to a room with a television and saw live footage of riots and tanks in the streets. The newscaster informed the public, in a severe and threatening tone, that many protestors had been jailed and more than a hundred killed. We knew our families in Austria were seeing this on the news, but when one of our guys picked up a phone to make a long-distance call, all the communications had been shut down. We still had time to leave the country, and the translator said, "If you guys stay here with the team, I will stay with you." One of us, I think it was Reid, said, "We are not going anywhere."

We suited up and went to the gym, where we spent the day training and working out with the national team. Then, in the late afternoon, we asked Eugene if we could meet with some of the wrestlers after dinner to talk about our faith. He said, "Yes, that is what I want you to do. I will arrange it." We thanked him and, after going to our rooms to wash up and change, we headed to the cafeteria for a hearty meal. At about seven o'clock, Eugene came to the cafeteria and said, "The boys are waiting!" We followed him down a hallway and up some steps, then down another hallway with a door at the end. We were expecting about a half-dozen guys at the most, but when we came to the room and Eugene opened the door, the whole team of about 30 wrestlers was there!

After we entered, Eugene left and closed the door. At first the athletes just stared at us, wondering what this meeting might really be about. Reid stood up in front and said, "We want to talk with you about Jesus Christ." When he said that, it seemed like the wrestlers all leaned forward in their chairs, eager to learn something they had heard about but never really known. Of course, they were probably all familiar with the rituals and formalities of the Catholicism known in their country, but as we started talking, sharing about the joy and meaningfulness of life in relationship with Christ, they kept their eyes glued to whoever was speaking.

For a full hour, we talked about the total athlete, the physical, mental and spiritual. We shared the Four Laws, using illustrations from wrestling and other sports. As the heavyweight, I used my grip illustration to show the importance of getting a hold on the Bible. "You have to grip it in your mind," I told them, "just like you grip someone's leg or arm in a match." They stared at me wide-eyed as I explained with passion, "God made us in His image, and if the spiritual is not the foundation, your whole identity as a person is in the prison of your athletic performance. But if you have a relationship with Jesus Christ, you are freed from that prison, and all of your training and competition as an athlete is an offering to God who loves you, whether you win or lose on the mat."

I emphasized winning is very important, and every good athlete goes out there to do his best with the goal of winning. Then, I added, "But if you offer it all to God through Christ, with love as your strongest motivation, you have even more energy and determination because nothing is stronger than love." At times, as I stared in their eyes, they seemed astonished to see a heavyweight wrestler speaking of love as the strongest motivation, and honoring Christ as the highest goal.

After an hour had passed, we figured it was enough for them, but they told us, "No! We want more!" We laughed with joy, and Reid told them, "Okay, we can do another hour." We started telling them about living in the power of the Holy Spirit, and an hour later, one of us said, "Okay, let's take a break." They all leaned forward and motioned with their hands, saying, "We don't need a break!" We told them, "Maybe you don't need a break, but we do!" They agreed to five minutes, and after we went for two more hours. Those young athletes were full of questions, and the translator did a great job. When we finally called it a night, they said they would be waiting for us after dinner the next day!

They were not joking. They held us to it. Every night that week, we sat in the room with almost the entire team, wearing out the translator with hours of sharing, teaching, questions and answers. We left Poland amazed at the doors God had opened, and the life-changing results of our evangelism and discipleship. We prayed the athletes would take back to their homes, their families, and their communities, the excitement and power of what they had learned in Zakopane.

Doug, Steve, John, Reid, and Carl in Vienna

Noreen and me with our children, along with 7-foot Polish wrestler Adam Sandursky and lightweight wrestler Jan Flandis

CHAPTER NINE
Wrestling and Witnessing

——

"For God so loved the world"

(JOHN 3:16)

In January of 1982, the Director of a Bible college in Schladming, Austria, invited us to do a demonstration during the week of competitions at the Alpine Ski World Championships. In front of over a thousand people we did a presentation that featured a wrestling demonstration, juggling, a comedy pro wrestling skit, all interspersed with testimonies and sharing the Gospel.

Using the love of sports to share with ski fans

After our last day at the championships, we attended an evangelistic meeting held in German at the nearby Bible college. I was not feeling well that day, and had nearly decided to stay back in my room. After the Gospel presentation, the director said, "I would like you to turn to someone next to you and ask if they have any questions." A young Austrian woman turned to me and said what she had heard was interesting, and could I explain a little more? I had a booklet in German, an adapted version of the Four Spiritual Laws. I had never gone through the whole Gospel with someone in German, but God worked through my effort and this young woman prayed to receive Christ. We then went over some key points on the next steps of spiritual growth. Afterwards, I reflected on how I had almost decided not to attend, but God directed me sit next to this person who was ready to receive Christ. When I got home and told Noreen, she said something like, "This is why we moved to Europe!"

One day that summer, we were heading again to Poland for training, evangelism, and discipleship among those who had come to Christ since we began touring there. When we came to the border of Czechoslovakia, which we needed to pass on our way to Poland, an official noticed the picture on my passport showed me with a beard, but the one on my visa did not. He said, "This is a big problem. The pictures do not match. You cannot enter our country with a beard." Well, I was not going to let a beard keep me from going with my team. I pulled a razor from my luggage, and after a few minutes of searching for shaving cream, I shrugged and headed back on foot, razor in hand, to the border station in Austria about two hundred yards behind us. Wouldn't you know, there was no hot water at the station. What a great opportunity to practice what I preach, doing everything as unto the Lord. I did my best to keep a positive attitude while shaving off the beard, and later I even managed a smile as the guards waved us through.

Near the end of that summer, Doug and his family moved to Colorado Springs, where he would head up recruiting for AIA Europe. Doug had been my workout partner and a good friend since I joined AIA seven years earlier, and Noreen and I would really miss him and his family. By that time, Tom had already moved back to the States and would later become chaplain for the Minnesota Vikings, so the only remaining families from the original Vienna team were the Lampheres and us. The Lord soon blessed us with Don Shuler, another Olympic-level wrestler, who joined us with his wife and child after Doug had left.

Between Thanksgiving and Christmas, we wrestled and shared in Hungary, France, Czechoslovakia, and Poland. In late January we did a two-week evangelistic tour through West Germany and presented 15 programs, all sponsored by local churches, to over 3,000 people. Wherever we went, we always made clear we were there to support the local churches and ministry groups.

Austria poster for Wrestling Demonstration with
Olympic Champion John Peterson

I only went for the first week of that tour, because on February 10th, 1983, Noreen gave birth to our third amazing child, whom we named

Stephen Daniel. Stephen came in at 9 pounds and 11 ounces, and that was a very difficult birth for Noreen. Seeing what my wife went through to bring us that big bundle of joy left a lasting impression in my memory, and raised even more the level of appreciation I have for my wife. When it was all done, we thanked God for His gift of another child added to our home. We were also grateful for our neighbor, Ron Nelson, who babysat Elisabeth and David while I was with Noreen in the hospital.

In May, our team went to Israel for the multi-sport Hapoel Games, a sort of mini-Olympics where thousands of athletes from 26 countries competed in front of friendly crowds. That was one of the four different times I wrestled in Israel during the mid-1980s. When we marched into the stadium at opening ceremonies, it was really a nice experience to look around at 20,000 people welcoming us with loud cheers. We waved back to them in acknowledgement of our gratitude, and then we got busy seeing who we could pin to the mat. Steve Barrett and I each won a gold medal in our respective weight classes, and Reid won a bronze in his.

USA Delegation at the Opening Ceremonies of the Hapoel Games in Israel

After the tournament, Noreen and baby Stephen joined me for a weeklong vacation, seeing places like Nazareth and Jerusalem. We spent an entire day at the home of Alex, the Israeli coach I had met in Madrid. He and his wife showed an openness to our sharing about the Bible and Messiah, and we had a nice time with them.

Meanwhile, back in Vienna, we had moved into the first floor of a house owned by a church. For Noreen and me, this was our first time not living in an apartment since we married. With the space capabilities of our new home, every Tuesday we had about 15 kids over from the Vienna International School, eating lots of snacks and having a great time. The kids were from countries which included New Zealand, the Philippines, Nigeria, Palestine, Egypt, Italy and America. After some time of games, we all sat down for a Bible study. What a joy to see how God had brought these kids from all over the world to become friends and learn together about Christ right there in our home.

The year 1983 brought a special memory for Elisabeth. In June, and then again in August, we went to Bulgaria where we stayed in a hotel by the Black Sea. Each evening and night I had ministry to attend to, but the kids had all day, every day, to hang out on the beach. The really interesting part came in the following year, when Elisabeth attended a children's Sunday School class during our furlough to the U.S. At one point, the teacher said to Elisabeth, "What is your favorite country?" She answered, "Bulgaria!" The teacher paused for a moment, aware most of the kids in the class did not even know where Bulgaria was on a map, but Elisabeth had carried the memory of our times there from the previous summer. The teacher who told us about this thought it was the cutest thing.

On another trip to Bulgaria, this time with AIA teammates, we met two world champion acrobats named Matt and Flip, who were twins and very strong believers. They also had jobs as national athletic coaches in different sports. During their exhibitions, Flip stood on Matt's shoulders and amazed the crowd by doing flips. They used the attraction, and their positions as coaches, to carefully probe other Bulgarians for an openness to talk about spiritual things. When we met with other believers from the youth group in the local church, we walked far out into the woods where we prayed together and worshiped, and I did my illustration of getting a grip on the Bible. We explained how sports can be used to share the Gospel, and also how God can be worshiped through our love for sports.

One time we went to Matt and Flip's apartment for a mini-conference under the cover of night, to encourage them to continue taking steps of faith in a difficult environment. The sad thing was after we left, my acrobat friends were called in by the authorities and told, "You have been meeting with a big American who lives in Europe and has a beard." The police told them I worked for the CIA (which I actually did, except the letters stood for *Christians in Action!*), and if they ever met with me again, they would be removed from their jobs and forbidden to leave the country.

In 1983, the world wrestling championships were held in Kyiv (formerly known as Kiev). The U.S. national team was training in Budapest, and John Peterson, only a few hours away in Vienna, was asked to come down and to help with coaching. When the day came for us to make the drive to Ukraine, since there were about 10 of us, we used two vehicles. John and his dad were in our van, along with Reid, Ron Nelson, and a Christian baseball player named Tom Simms. About an hour behind us was Don Zellmer, riding with Steve and Cindi Barrett in their VW Bug.

After driving all day, we stopped at the Ukrainian border a little before sunset. Since we knew there would be a scarcity of fresh fruit in Kyiv, we had brought 44 pounds of bananas and 24 liters of fruit juice for the U.S. national team, who would be arriving by train. Well, when the border guards looked through our stuff, they pointed to the bananas and said, "This is a very big problem. It is against the law to bring bananas into our country." In a situation like this, there is really not much a traveler can do. We tried reasoning with the guards, but they held firm and told us we could eat as many as we wanted before crossing, but we could not take the fruit into their country. After discussing this among ourselves, we decided to have a banana eating contest. John and I tied for the lead by eating eight bananas each! As I was forcing down my eighth and last, a chilly breeze stirred a swirl of leaves at my feet, and I looked out toward the sun dipping in the west. Just a few years earlier,

I was a young wrestler touring the eastern USA, and I could not have imagined standing with a group of athletes eating bananas at a border crossing to the Soviet Union.

After we had gone through all of that, the guards were amazed we had eaten so many, and they ended up taking a few pounds for their families, letting us keep the rest!

At the championships, a coach named Nick had a Russian wrestling book he was trying to trade for a Playboy magazine. When he approached me speaking very good English, I told him, "I don't have a Playboy, but I have a booklet that has been very helpful to me." After he shrugged and nodded, I said, "Would you like to go somewhere for lunch? I'll pay." Well, he was not going to turn down a free lunch, so next thing he knew, he was sitting at a restaurant table with me and a few others from AIA, eating a good meal while we talked with him about Jesus. I was actually surprised at how open he was, and he gave his full attention as we walked him through *The Four Spiritual Laws*. After our meal and conversation, we went our separate ways.

The next day in the arena, Nick sought me out in the late afternoon and said he would like to speak with me in private. We found a quiet spot where Nick told me he wanted to hear more. After a short time of sharing my testimony and answering some questions, Nick prayed to receive Christ. The next day, as he and I were talking, I asked him what had done the most to persuade him to receive Jesus. He explained he spent five years in prison for petty crimes, and there was a Baptist pastor serving time for preaching the Gospel too boldly. Nick had noticed how the pastor and other Christians in the prison carried themselves differently, not showing fear or anger but rather kindness, patience, and other positive qualities. Nick said as he watched and listened to us, we reminded him of the pastor he had seen in prison. That was quite a lesson for me, to be reminded of how we never know who the Spirit might be urging to watch us and put our testimony to the test. Displays of anger, cheating, or something like having pornography can damage a long-term testimony in just a few seconds.

Reid and Carl with Ukrainian wrestling coach Nick
(center) at 1983 World Championships in Kyiv

In June we visited family in Philadelphia and then in Auburn, from where I flew to Los Angeles for the Olympics. I had decided not to try out for the U.S. team. I probably could have wrestled for Austria, since I was a three-time national champ there, having won in two styles in 1983 and one in 1984. But Austria had a rule which required Olympians to live in the country for at least three years after the competitions. We had enjoyed our five years in Vienna.

But a big move was about to happen...

CHAPTER TEN

Germany

___

"Call to Me, and I will show you great and mighty things."
(JEREMIAH 33:3)

By 1984, the consensus among Cru leadership was for a need to decentralize in Europe. The years of clustering in Vienna were ending, and each family had to make its decision. Some went back to the U.S., some to England, some had good reasons for staying in Vienna, but most decided on a move to Starnberg, a beautiful German city near the mountains south of Munich. Noreen and I, along with our AIA teammates, decided against this, mainly because it was not a wrestling area. After some scouting, we chose a small village called Hallbergmoos, about thirty minutes north of Munich.

Reid and his family moved there in January. After meeting with the president of the local wrestling club, Reid learned wrestling was a weekly highlight in the town. When he told the team about me and our plan to relocate, the president sent word that he was coming down to Vienna with a large truck to pack and haul our belongings to our new home. We were leaving a metropolis for a town of three-thousand, and everyone knew the Americans were moving in. When we arrived in Hallbergmoos on October 15th, we got a hero's welcome from the local wrestling club.

The Lord blessed us to rent a nice house in a duplex next to a large field of vegetables. The area was residential but spread out with large open spaces between the homes, with our teammates living on the same country block a few hundred yards away. By that time, Elisabeth was ready to start kindergarten, and the school was only a five-minute walk away, with a wrestling hall right next to it! We also found an evangelical, German-speaking church about 10 miles away, with nearly 70 regular members, half of whom were students. In Munich, we found an international, English-speaking church pastored by an American named Ronnie Stevens. What a wonderful place to raise a family, and the kids were excited to look out from our yard and see cows, sheep, and geese. Sometimes I would stop and look around with amazement at where God had brought us.

Ten days after the move to Germany, I was with Reid and the guys in Bulgaria, the first communist country I had wrestled in during the 1977 trip with Bud Hinkson, Steve Barrett, Don Shuler, Reid, Don Zellmer, and John Peterson. We spent a weekend there, doing training and covert discipling with athletes and students we had built relationships with during our years of operating out of Vienna. What an encouragement to see young people with open hearts in a country dominated for almost half a century by the ruthless policies of atheistic communism.

The same year, we were joined in Hallbergmoos by AIA member Doug Radunzel, who came from the U.S. with his family. The neighbors in general were very nice to us, and we developed many wonderful friendships, but it was great to have the inner circle of AIA families where we could all understand and encourage each other.

In November of 1984, Noreen and the kids came with me for a Sports Missionary Congress near Frankfurt, spearheaded by a German ministry called *Sportler ruft Sportler* (*Sportsmen Calling Sportsmen*), working closely with AIA. This was the first of its kind, and the purpose

The new AIA team of Reid, Doug Radunzel, Carl, Ray Caldwell, and Steve Mousetis

was to discuss our vision for a wide-reaching, coordinated sports ministry for all of Europe. We had always engaged in partnerships with others for tours and events, even back in the U.S., but we were realizing the advantage of joining forces in a more organized way with like-minded ministries. More than a hundred German-speaking Christian sports people from four different countries attended. We prayed with them, worshiped together, enjoyed friendly sports competitions, and talked about the steps for building local sports ministries for evangelism and discipleship.

Helping to facilitate this vision was a sports movement aimed at helping to develop sports ministries around the world. This network provided encouragement, furthered partnerships, pooled resources, and helped everyone work together regionally and globally.

AIA was the first to send out full-time teams of Christian athletes organizing tours in various sports throughout the country and expanding internationally. God had abundantly blessed our work, in North America and Europe, but we wanted to help other countries develop sports ministries among their own nationals. There was no manual for how to do this, to build a national sports ministry from the ground up, but we were learning. So, we began inviting church leaders and Christian sportspersons to conferences. That 1984 Congress near Frankfurt was a significant step toward what we have today.

In 1967, Dave Hannah, John Klein, Larry Amundson, Gene Davis, Greg Hicks, Bob Anderson and a handful of others stepped out in faith toward the goal of building a ministry that used sports as a platform for sharing the Gospel and teaching life skills on a spiritual foundation. They could not have imagined how the Holy Spirit was going to guide and develop the 1960s effort into a globally organized network of partnerships.

Meanwhile, back at home, one of my first competitive events was a friendly match against a club from Austria, held outdoors in a beer garden under a tent. The organizers put tables together with mats on top, along with other tables loaded with food and drinks. It was one of the most unique wrestling events I have ever been in. A couple weeks later, my parents visited for Christmas, and it was great for the children to experience the love and attention of grandparents. After five years in the Vienna metropolis, we were enjoying the rural life of Hallbergmoos.

My schedule in the months after Christmas included a week in the Polish national training camp, a 10-day tour through Tbilisi, Kyiv and Moscow, a week of competition in Israel, 10 days with the Czechoslovakian team, various outreaches in Germany and Switzerland, and a week-long AIA team ski retreat in Austria. From there, we went to Berlin for Expo '85, a worldwide conference for prayer and missions, where I led two seminars on how to use sports as a platform to share the Gospel. After all of that came the *really* big event—our beautiful daughter Elisabeth lost her first tooth!

Our family in the Alps where Noreen was a good skier

Every year the AIA Europe Team would spend a week in Austria skiing and planning ministry activities

In ministry, although our heart was for the communist world, we did a lot of work in Central Europe. Our first partnership was with an evangelistic ministry called Operation Mobilization in Austria, whose leaders would invite us and then advertise an Olympic level exhibition. As word about us spread, the leadership of the YMCA in Germany invited us to do outreaches. Also, we continued to partner with *Sportler ruft Sportler* (SRS) and an English organization called *Christians in Sport* (CIS). Working together with these and other ministries and churches, we spoke at rallies and provided wrestling demonstrations with as many as 7,000 in attendance. The fact that I had flunked Level Three German in high school, and was now traveling through European countries sharing with tens of thousands in that very language, illustrated how God uses people based on their availability, not necessarily on their ability.

AIA team on stage at Stuttgart's Center Square for a "Jesus Festival"

Carl lifting a teammate before sharing with the audience
about the strength that comes from Christ

A crowd in Germany enjoy a demonstration of
wrestling while hearing the Good News

A crowd hears the gospel after demonstrations
of strength, agility and wrestling

The AIA leaders back in Colorado Springs were doing a great job of recruiting teams of Christian athletes from various sports. The athletes themselves were excited about traveling through European countries, not only competing, but also sharing their faith and seeing lands they had only heard about. Our job was to accommodate and orient the players and their coaches to the cultures they would be encountering, and to help with preparation, travel arrangements, and ministry follow-up after they left. In those missionary sports tours, not only did thousands of Europeans hear the Gospel preached in a personal way, but the lives of U.S. athletes were transformed as they appreciated more the benefits of living in the U.S., and gained a vision for how God could use their love for sports as a way of ministry. Many of them started praying for the countries they had toured.

In August of 1986, my brother Bob and his family visited on their way back to the States after their second three-year term as missionaries in Nigeria. It was great for the cousins to be together, and for all of them to see some of the places where we did ministry.

From Left, David, Stephen, Tom, Ben and
Elisabeth on our couch in Germany

In early 1987, I talked with Reid about the idea of a European
Christian Sports Conference, which would aim to provide athletes
with training in discipleship, provide church leaders with know-how
for teaming with Christian athletes for building sports ministries in
their areas, and move more strongly toward organizing sports ministry
partnerships throughout western and eastern Europe. Reid liked the
idea, and we began contacting leaders of established organizations, all
of whom agreed to partner with AIA-Europe in setting this up. This
conference, which we decided to call *Arena*, would become a major step
toward forming the European Christian Sports Union.

God blessed our work in putting together the pieces, and in October
we held a conference in Austria, with almost 60 ministry leaders from
20 European countries. We accomplished a lot, providing training in
how to develop sports ministry, and helping those leaders realize how
God was building a network across the continent. The conference really
boosted confidence, vision, and momentum.

A month later in Hungary, we had our first official AIA *Eastern
European Sports Ministry Conference*. Three Olympic champions
from different sports (John Peterson, Papp Laszlo, and Andros Baltso)
shared their testimonies with guys from Russia, Poland, Hungary, and

Czechoslovakia. Bud Hinkson also was there as the main speaker. I was gaining administrative experience and building international relationships and trust, just at the time my competitive career was winding down. As always, God was working out the next phase of His plan.

European sports ministry leaders gathered in Austria

Three Olympic champions (John Peterson, Papp Laszlo, and Andros Balczo) shared their testimonies at the conference in Hungary

CHAPTER ELEVEN
Tear Down This Wall!

"Rejoice with those who rejoice; mourn with those who mourn."
(ROMANS 12:15)

One day in early February of 1988 we received an emergency call from Noreen's family. The home of her sister, Sharon, had caught fire by sparks from a wood stove. Sharon's husband had already left for work and the two older children had gone to school, but of the three children at home, the two youngest, Crystal (8) and Erin (5), died from smoke inhalation. Hearing the fire truck sirens, Noreen's dad had run for half-a-mile to get there, only to helplessly watch his grandchildren being loaded into an ambulance where the medical staff would make a heroic but unsuccessful effort to keep them alive.

We quickly had Noreen on a plane, where she was grateful to have an empty seat next to her as she cried through much of the flight. When she landed in Seattle, there was really nothing she could do except to bring presence and prayer, and to "weep with those who weep." It was like the flood that took away seven of the Cru women near Fort Collins in 1976. What can anyone say to bring comfort in times like those? We learn to accept, trust, and keep walking with God. To this day, my wife cannot talk about the experience without her voice breaking. It really hurt that bad. Those are experiences which help us pause and realize how precious life is.

Six months after that agonizing family tragedy, we were all in Oregon, at a resort for a family reunion. In the early-morning hours of our second day, the high-pitched sound of smoke alarms jolted us from sleep. The room next to ours on the third floor had caught fire, and there was only enough time to flee for our lives in pajamas. Thankfully, nobody was hurt, but we lost all of our material belongings, including the keys to our vehicles. The August fire was a hurtful experience, but it seemed to actually help Sharon understand how disasters can happen so quickly and unexpectedly that all we can do is our best in the moment.

Noreen stayed for a while with family, while I left in September to meet Reid in Seoul for a global congress on sport the week before the Summer Olympics. For ten days, more than five hundred pastors and sports leaders from 102 countries gathered in a hotel for training, workshops, fellowship, planning, and worship. The main objectives were to train people in how to use sports for sharing their faith, how to build local and nationwide sports ministries, and how to organize and do chaplaincy at major sporting events. Reid and I led a workshop on doing sports ministry in closed countries, and it was a special joy to see some of the guys we worked with in Eastern Europe.

Some of those who came to the congress were experienced church leaders, but they did not understand sports. We advised them, as a first step in building a sports ministry, to ask God for help in finding a Christian sportsperson to be the ambassador for their country. Before the congress had ended, a decision was made to have one every four years in the region where the Olympics would be held. These meetings would involve a coalition of sports ministries aiming to help local churches prepare to take advantage of the tremendous outreach opportunities when people came to their area from all over the world. Along with this, AIA began planning what we would call our *Olympic Project*, focusing mainly on ministry to those participating in the competitions (the "Olympic Family" of athletes, coaches, trainers, etc.).

The congress in Seoul overlapped with the first week of the Summer Olympics, in which I was invited to work with the chaplains inside the Village on two occasions. That was my first taste of chaplaincy-type work among athletes in a global, multi-sport environment, and I felt good in the position. I also got to watch some great wrestling matches, including seeing Aleksander Karelin win his first Olympic gold medal and personally meeting him.

The next big event was our long-planned, seven-day Arena Christian Sports Conference in Austria, with over 200 people in attendance, 42 of them coming from closed countries. That time of spiritual training and planning was a cooperative effort with multiple European organizations. Each day, the delegates could choose from among different seminars, all designed to give them practical help in developing a sports ministry in their own countries. The 1988 congress and the 1989 Arena Conference were two major events which catapulted the growth of partnerships and networking for the spread of the Gospel through sports.

By the Fall of 1989, things were changing fast in areas behind the collapsing Iron Curtain. Meanwhile, back at home, Noreen was asked to be chairwoman of our area's annual women's conference. Along with her ministry responsibilities, we were hosting a lot of people in our home, meaning she was up late at night with guests, then up early in the morning with the children. She handled it all with grace as the Lord enabled her, and in our prayer letter from that time, she jokingly wrote, "I am beginning to wonder if there is such a thing as a 'normal' life!"

Our team rolled on like an accelerating train, with no end in sight for the expanding opportunities. We had come to Europe with the goal of using sports as a cover for access to people in communist countries, and as a bridge into the lives of people in western countries where Christianity, understood as a personal relationship with Christ, had largely become a relic of the past. Over the years of that first decade, God enabled us to share His love in places we never imagined we would set foot in.

In early February of 1990, we did a follow-up journey through eastern Europe, where we met with and encouraged wrestlers in Romania, Hungary, Poland, Bulgaria, and even East Germany (formerly the toughest of all places for access). John Peterson led a wrestling clinic for a hundred Hungarian wrestling coaches, while three other teammates went to Transylvania with a van full of food, clothing, medicines, and hundreds of Christian books to distribute while sharing the Gospel. In each country, we met with sports leaders and discipleship groups, and in the evenings we spoke at churches and other venues. One of the large churches in Hungary was packed with over 2,500 people, and in the capital of Budapest we did our evangelistic program for 200 students at a college.

During our trip to East Germany, as we passed through Berlin, we saw the infamous Wall already partly torn down. I got out of the van, stepped past a barrier, then climbed a few feet up the Wall and used all the strength of my wrestler's grip to pull down a chunk of concrete which I carried back to the van.

Carl with a chunk of the Berlin Wall near *Checkpoint Charlie*

From Europe, we went on to a 12-day ministry trip in the Soviet Union, where I gave a 90-minute speech at the Sports University in Moscow, and we did our evangelistic wrestling program in a gym with 400 people. From there, we flew to Tbilisi, where we met with the mayor and discussed bringing an AIA baseball team to Soviet Georgia. We also had meetings with leaders in the Communist Party, Youth Organization, Sport Committee and Friendship Society, all of whom showed interest in

Christian sports teams and coaches coming into their areas. The person who opened those doors was Gogi, who had prayed to receive Christ through our ministry in 1983. We then spent several days back in Kyiv, where Nick, the guy who came looking for a Playboy and ended up with a Bible, along with a former bodybuilder named Alex, opened doors, and Ronnie Stevens came from Munich to preach the main message at a Ukrainian Baptist church.

During the tour through the Soviet Union, we found many open doors for evangelism and discipleship. A great highlight for me was the follow-up with a baseball player named Andy, who had received Christ in the previous year. Andy wanted me to share Christ with his friend and teammate, Sasha, so we all agreed to meet up at the recently built McDonalds next to Pushkinskaya Square. This was the largest McDonalds in the world, the first one ever in the Soviet Union. Steve Mousetis, who had joined us in Hallbergmoos in 1988, came with me. When we got to the location, we saw a line beginning at the entrance and stretching back in a loop around the south end of the park. From there, all along the wide, tree-lined sidewalk, stretching for hundreds of yards on the far end, people stood crowded together, waiting for the line to inch forward. Steve and I walked in silent amazement, listening to the crunch of our shoes in the snow. Finally, we came to a designated spot where we saw Andy and Sasha, both of them looking like Americans with their baseball hats, jackets, and tennis shoes. After the four of us greeted, Andy leaned in close and said, "I know how to sneak in through the back." I told him, "No, let's be good sportsmen and play by the rules." That got a laugh from everyone as we made our way to the end of a line which stretched so far it seemed like it might fall off the edge of the city.

We started with small talk about baseball and sports in general. After a few minutes, I asked Andy to share how he had come to believe, and as he started talking, I noticed Sasha watching intently. When Andy finished, Sasha nodded, stayed quiet for a second, then turned to me and said in halting English, "I want to know Christ. Can you help me better understand?"

What a perfect opportunity for sharing the Gospel. We had a young Russian athlete, hungry for a double cheeseburger, fries and a milkshake, but needing to stand in line for at least another hour! I started by taking him through *The Four Spiritual Laws* and answering his questions on certain points. Sasha was all ears as he soaked up the Good News about Jesus, and before we got to the entrance, he prayed and gave his life to Christ. A few minutes later, we walked through the doors into the restaurant and ordered our food. Steve and I had to leave, but we assured them we would get together again the next time we came to Moscow. That experience with the baseball players has gone down in my personal history as "The Cheeseburger Evangelism Story"!

Carl with Russian baseball players Sasha and Andy at McDonalds

When I got back to Germany, Noreen rejoiced with excitement as I told her story after story about the doors Christ had opened for the Gospel. I said, "Sweetheart, there is incredible spiritual hunger in the lands of the Soviet Union." We agreed that the harvest was ripe and the laborers few (cf. Matthew 9:38), and we both knew the time had come to start talking about a possible move to Moscow.

Later that day, I took the large chunk of concrete from the Berlin

Wall, broke it into smaller pieces, and put it in the back of the garage for our next trip to the U.S., where I would give the pieces as souvenirs to some of our supporters.

Over the next few days and weeks, everyone on the team seemed to be of one mind about the new phase. We had come to a time of unprecedented opportunities for discipleship among those we had evangelized in communist countries, and although our home life in Germany was comfortable, we knew God was calling us deeper into the fields of harvest. Different families began praying which country the Lord would have them move to for new discipleship and evangelistic opportunities.

For Noreen and me, the big question in prayer became, "Lord, will You use us in Russia even if we do not know the language?" Russian is a difficult language, and we were not even confident we *could* learn it. We had worked so hard to learn German, and for six years had lived in a peaceful village among pleasant neighbors, with plenty of ministry opportunities and a very stable life for our kids. Did we *really* want to leave all of that and bring our children into the unknown hazards of a large city with a language and culture we did not know? We listened patiently for His voice as we prayed, "Show us, Lord, if this is where You are calling our family."

For the next six months, the idea of a move to Moscow gained momentum. From a ministry standpoint, it made sense, as it would mean less travel time and more opportunity for local evangelism and discipleship. Why keep traveling east out of Germany when we could now openly share in some of the countries where the secret police had previously followed us almost everywhere? Also, from the standpoint of family, it would mean doing more ministry closer to home instead of so frequently being away.

In May of 1990, Noreen and I traveled to Moscow and Tbilisi. We had not come on a mere "visit," but rather on a scouting mission to get a feel for what to expect. We had not yet made a final decision, but we believed the Lord would give a decisive answer.

On our first full day there, out in Red Square a young man approached and said, "Hello," surprising us with a greeting in our language. I said, "We hope you speak English, because we do not know

Russian!" He glanced around with a furtive look, then adjusted his cap and proceeded to tell us his name was Yuri, and he had learned English mainly from illegally listening to radio broadcasts from the BBC and VOA. We felt amazed at his determination and alertness to opportunity, and after a few minutes of small talk we asked him what he knew about Jesus Christ. "I have heard about Him," he said, "but I would like to learn more."

We talked for a while, not sure if he was truly interested in Christ, or if he just relished the opportunity of speaking with Americans. When we told him we needed to be going, he nodded graciously and asked for a phone number where he could reach us. I gave him the number for our hotel room, then we said goodbye and went our ways.

The next day, Yuri called, asking questions about Christ. I talked with him a while, sharing my personal testimony and taking him through *The Four Spiritual Laws*. He said he was thinking seriously about these things, and as we ended, he thanked me for the call. Over the next week, both in Moscow and in Tbilisi, every day the Lord led us to someone with whom we shared Christ in English. I am not exaggerating. Every single day. For seven decades, the people in that part of the world had been spiritually oppressed by an aggressive form of atheistic communism, and many a Christian had disappeared into the Siberian labor camps where only God and all of heaven know how they finished their years on earth. Now, all of a sudden, we could walk through those lands sharing Christ without the nationals needing to worry about a knock on the door in the middle of the night.

After our time in Georgia, we came back to Russia for our last day in Moscow. In the evening after dinner, Noreen jokingly said, "You know, we haven't shared our faith with anybody in English today." Less than two minutes later, the phone rang. I picked up the receiver and barely had time to say "Hello" before Yuri broke in and said, "Please, tell me one more time about this Jesus Christ." I must have been grinning from ear to ear as I walked this young man through what he needed to understand about trusting Christ as his Lord and Savior. After that call, my beautiful wife and I knew God had given His answer. Moscow would be our new home.

In our prayer letter from July of that year, Noreen poured out her heart to family and supporters back in the USA:

> "So many times we like to avoid difficulties, but it seems that is the very point where we see God's intervention on our behalf, which in turn encourages us and helps us to trust Him more. Our trip to the USSR really did confirm in both Carl and I that moving there is what the Lord would have us do…On the last night [in Moscow], Carl spent over an hour on the phone, mostly answering [a young man's] questions about Jesus. His name is Yuri, please pray for him."

Meanwhile, the amazing and rapid political changes allowed us to schedule and present, on June 10, an evangelistic wrestling program for 5,000 young people in East Berlin! A month later, our good friends Reid and Carolyn moved with their children to Prague, to focus on discipleship ministry among those who had come to Christ through our ministry there. Don Zellmer and his family had already settled in Poland for the same reason, and Doug Radunzel with his family was planning to eventually join us in Moscow. All around us, we were seeing this fruitful and memorable chapter in our lives come to a close. There was a touch of sadness to this, of course. We knew we would miss the people and the times in Germany, but we saw so much spiritual potential in moving to Moscow, very similar to our decision to leave the USA for Europe back in 1979.

CHAPTER TWELVE

Moscow

——

"Who am I, O LORD God, and what is my
family, that You have brought me this far?"
(1 CHRONICLES 17:16)

I n July of 1990, I was asked to serve as a chaplain at the Goodwill Games in Seattle, with 2,500 athletes from 50 countries. This was my first time serving as an official chaplain in a multi-sport, international event. I shared and prayed with many of the athletes, gave Bibles in different languages, and also met President Reagan in a brief but memorable encounter. One beautiful summer day I was walking next to a baseball diamond with my friend, Norm Evans, the head of Pro Athletes Outreach and a two-time Super Bowl champion for the Miami Dolphins. As we talked, Andy and Sasha from Russia saw us and stopped, just as I was telling Norm about our plans to move to Moscow. After they had listened for a minute, Andy suddenly held up both hands and said, "No, do not move to Moscow! Come and visit Moscow, but do not move there!" Norm looked at me, indicating with his expression that maybe I should consider what we had just heard. I shrugged and said, "My wife and I believe God is leading us there."

With Norm Evans, who mentored and encouraged
me in my walk with the Lord

After coming home, I wrestled against West Germany's national teenage champion. Some of my friends were there, enjoying the opportunity to see a young athlete on the rise compete against an experienced 40-year-old. How would it turn out? Well, I ended up beating the kid, but whereas he walked off the mat with a steady stride, I almost had to crawl off! I won by using my old man skills, like getting an underhook and stalling, but by the end of the match, it felt like somebody had sucked all the air from the arena. Between the time-investments of ministry and raising three kids at home, I could no longer give what was needed for maintaining the conditioning required for competition. I made the decision and let it be known, "That was my last match."

Something every athlete has to eventually face is the time when he or she can no longer perform at the previous level. That is one of those places where the spiritual foundation becomes so important. My retirement from competition came just at the time I was being asked to serve internationally in multi-sport chaplaincy, and my training as a total athlete served me well in those positions. Under the hard realities of competition at an international level, young athletes sometimes seek out guidance, and as a chaplain I was there to bring presence and point them to higher levels of motivation and reward.

On December 4, 1990, we finished packing up and left Hallbergmoos for the last time. We sent our furniture and food separately, then drove to the coast of northern Germany, put our car on a ferry and crossed the sea to Finland, where friends of Ron Nelson hosted us for two days. From there, since the roads at that time of year were not safe for driving with three kids, we had our car loaded onto a train which took us to Moscow, a city unlike any in which we had ever lived.

In our previous moves, to Austria and Germany, we entered the new land accompanied by AIA teammates. The move to Moscow was different. There were American Cru members in the city, but none from AIA, and even the nearest Cru families lived more than a half-hour away. Our friends in Moscow had contracted on our behalf with a guy who ran a language-learning institute, and the deal was for him to get us a visa, an apartment, and a language helper for up to 40 hours a week. After some initial complications at the apartment on the sixth floor of a high-rise, we managed to get settled into our new home. In our prayer letter from that month, Noreen wrote, "At our two-bedroom flat, you just have to ignore the smell and appearance of the common halls and elevators on the way up. This is our month of no hot water."

The first goals in Moscow were learning the basics, like how to get food, find a school for the kids, find a church, get started in the language program, and find where the local sports teams trained. We got to Russia during a difficult time, when finding food like meat, eggs and cheese was more like hunting and gathering than shopping. One day in a store I spotted roasted chickens and stood in line for nearly an hour, only to watch the guy in front of me get the last one. The good thing was we could always find items like bread, cabbage and milk, and the stores had a good stock of mineral water that came in three flavors (rust flavor, sulfur flavor, and salt flavor). Nice to have a selection.

Visiting AIA members often brought suitcases full of goodies such as chocolate chips, tortillas, and refried beans, and we also had access to western foods from a catalog at the U.S. Embassy. Now and then we splurged from the catalog, loading up on canned goods and other non-perishables. Meanwhile, Noreen and I also had a private language teacher named Larissa, who came to our apartment for the lessons and helped with general survival information about life in Moscow. From the beginning, she was open to the Gospel, and before long we were using more time sharing with her about Christ and the Bible than studying Russian!

A month after we got to Moscow, the city celebrated Christmas publicly for the first time in seven decades. We stood with the Russians in Red Square for the candlelight service in below-zero weather. *Nightline*, with Ted Koppel, had the cameras rolling, and people in the

U.S. and Western Europe watched from their homes as the Russians joyfully sang hymns while holding candles against the backdrop of a giant, lit-up Christmas Tree. At one point, the *Nightline* camera zoomed in on Noreen and Stephen. As the camera crew filmed the mother beside her bundled up child who clutched a burning candle in his tiny hand, they had no idea they were filming Americans. What a thrill for our family and supporters back home to see us celebrating with the Muscovites in Red Square. After the Russian

Christmas Candlelight Service on Red Square in 1990, with Saint Basil's Cathedral in background

service, we walked to the nearby McDonalds and splurged on some tasty American food!

AIA wrestlers dressed for warmth in Moscow

In January, John Peterson and Steve Barrett came to Moscow with another AIA wrestler. We did evangelistic outreaches, demonstrating different styles of wrestling while sharing the Gospel at schools and a community center. We also visited a university where the president asked for help in setting up a Sports and Bible Department. We found the people in general loved meeting Americans, and they were very open to talking about the Gospel. During that time with us in Russia, Steve decided he wanted to bring his family later in that year and live there. Ever since I had met him back in 1977, he showed a strong heart for reaching the unreachable with the Gospel, and God had put in him a passion to use his wrestling skills for mission work.

Meanwhile, we had enrolled the kids in the Anglo-American school run by the embassies of Canada, the U.S. and Australia. They attended that school from December through June of the first year, and we soon realized it would be way too expensive to keep sending them there. We were expecting many more missionaries and their families to join us in the coming years, and we saw it as imperative to provide a strong, affordable, college-prep education for all the kids. We spoke with several

Cru staff families who agreed to join in a team effort to open our own international school!

The Moscow team had to find a location, recruit teachers, and develop a curriculum. God blessed us to rent a classroom in a Russian school, then to have American teachers come and build a curriculum, and be there to start classes at *New Life Christian School* on opening day in September of 1991! There were 12 students at the start of the first semester, with classes taught in English. Initially, the school was only for kids connected to Cru, but a few years later we opened it to others. Helping to start the international Christian school was one of the biggest accomplishments God enabled us to do in Russia.

In November, Steve and Cindi with their children joined us, along with Ron Nelson from Budapest. Before they arrived, we scouted out apartments for them about a five-minute drive from us.

With Bill Bright and Bud and Shirley Hinkson
before our move to Russia

With the team in our first Moscow apartment. Bud
and Shirley Hinkson are on the far left

Meanwhile, rather than having Larissa come to our apartment, we
joined other Cru staff at a language school where we studied Russian
four days a week with professional instructors. We also hired a local
18-year-old named Nick, who had come to Christ through the Cru
ministry, to make daily food runs at American restaurants. Because he
had previously worked at McDonalds, we called him *McNick*, and we
paid him 20 dollars a month (the normal salary for a teacher or a factory
worker) to make runs to McDonalds on Mondays and Wednesdays,
and to Pizza Hut on Tuesdays and Thursdays. This helped to keep us
motivated, knowing after studying Russian for hours, McNick would be
there with some unhealthy but very tasty food.

Our main focus with AIA-Russia was on athletes and students. The
younger generation was more open, and we not only had a bridge to
them through sports, but we believed we could reach the older Russians
through their kids and grandkids. Most of those young people had never
heard the Gospel in a relationship way, and they were attending our
evangelistic sports demonstrations in large numbers, with many also
accepting invitations to small group Bible studies.

Although our normal policy in evangelizing was to point people
to existing, local churches, the situation in Moscow was unique. Many

of the churches had been through decades of persecution, and had developed a fortress mentality, holding firmly to the internal culture that had protected them from outside influences. All of a sudden, they were seeing young people responding to the Gospel and wanting a less restrictive, more joyful worship environment. The older generation seemed threatened by this, or at least uncomfortable with it, creating a difficult situation for the younger believers.

We knew we needed to disciple those kids, not just lead them to the faith and then hope they would grow. To do this, we had to provide a worship and fellowship environment where they could be themselves. As the number of younger people coming to our gatherings swelled, we partnered with Cru to start the *Moscow Bible Church*, asking Ronnie Stevens to come from Munich and serve as the first pastor. Ronnie preached in English, but everything was translated, and this attracted Russians who at first only came for the opportunity to sharpen their English, but who ended up hearing a message that changed their lives forever.

We also quickly began coordinating with other organizations to bring in Christian teams from the west. One of those was a soccer team called the Charlotte Eagles, who came to Moscow for the first time in June of 1991. The story of the Eagles unfolds into other important developments for the work of AIA throughout Russia and other former Soviet Republics. Two of the men on the initial tour were soccer player Tom Merchant and California businessman Bill Shubin.

Bill, who would become a major sponsor and traveler with AIA-Russia and beyond, had been in Moscow the previous year for reasons unrelated to sports. Bill is of Russian descent, speaks the language, and has a fascinating family history which includes a dramatic escape from a Stalinist labor camp in the early 1930s. During his 1990 visit, he paid for the printing of 5,000 Russian Bibles and other Christian literature, having no idea how he would put his investment to use. Just an act of faith, working on gut instinct and believing God had a purpose.

About nine months later, Bill was asked to accompany the Eagles as a translator during their planned 1991 tour. The main organizer for the tour was Brian Davidson, who mentioned in a call to Bill that the team needed Bibles for distribution during the evangelistic sports events. Bill blurted out, "I have the Bibles waiting in Moscow!" What an amazing glimpse of how God works behind the scenes, setting up the pieces for the Great Commission to move forward. Next thing we knew, Bill was introduced to us at the Moscow Airport as we welcomed the team.

Also coming off the plane was the young soccer player I have mentioned, Tom Merchant, whose life would be changed through his experience of touring and evangelizing in Russia and Ukraine. Seeing firsthand the enormous spiritual hunger and need in that part of the world, Tom felt his heart directed by Christ to become a full-time missionary, using his athletic talent as a platform to evangelize and disciple in places he never imagined he would set foot. Tom's missionary experience also unfolded into a beautiful romance story, as he fell in love with and married a Christian woman in Ukraine. He and his wife are now raising a family there, and Tom plays an active role in the development of local soccer ministries nationwide.

One of the challenges in those early years was Russian people seeing us as a possible way for a move to America. We had to keep up our guard, making clear we had come there to help initiate and build national sports ministries, not to help people get out of the country! "We need you here," I would tell them. This challenge of keeping Christian nationals in Russia led to an interesting situation with the generous-hearted Bill Shubin.

In Moscow, we had an excellent translator named Olga, married to a wonderful young man named Tony. During Bill's time in Moscow, he developed a warm relationship with the young couple and became a fatherly figure to them, even arranging for their move to the U.S.! A year later, when Bill came again with the Eagles, we all gathered in a large room where I briefed the team on what to expect during their time with us. I said, "You are going to meet some fantastic people, but please do not invite them to live in America, because we need them here, and especially those who know both languages." While I was talking, I looked several times directly at Bill. Finally, he politely interrupted, putting up his hands and saying emphatically, "I won't do it again." It was disappointing to lose Olga, but after that night at the briefing, we laughed it off.

The Charlotte Eagles soccer team had many outreaches
in the former USSR during the 1990s

On another occasion, Canadian ice hockey star Paul Henderson, who scored a sensational winning goal in a match against the Soviets in 1972, came to Moscow with a group of AIA-Canada members. We set up speaking opportunities for them at sports clubs and universities, and they had a big impact because of how ice hockey is such a major sport in Russia.

Another amazing development with an open door came in January of 1992, at a professional ice hockey tournament held in Leninsky Park. I had received a call from a journalist named Vladimir, asking if I would "do a blessing for the tournament." After assuring him I would be glad to do this, he left me speechless by saying the blessing would be aired on Soviet national television, meaning it would be heard and seen by over a hundred-million people! Vladimir then went on to say, "I would like you to sit in the VIP section, where Brezhnev used to watch the games, and you will be seated with Gordie Howe." After the call, I stood by the phone and reflected on how just a couple years earlier, we had been followed everywhere and had to speak with the nationals covertly about our faith.

A couple days later, I spoke to the Soviet people on camera for two minutes about competing for an imperishable prize. Using a paraphrase from 1 Corinthians 9:24-25, I said something like, "In ancient Greece,

Olympians got a wreath that fades away, but if we are living for God's glory, we get a wreath that lasts forever." After giving the blessing, my family and I were escorted to a lounge where we had a great time with Gordie, his wife, and a couple of their grandkids. It was a new era in Russia.

With NHL and Team Canada superstar Paul Henderson in Moscow

NHL legend Gordy Howe, "Mr. Hockey," with our
kids Elisabeth, David, and Stephen

CHAPTER THIRTEEN

Highs and Lows

———

*"The Lord upholds all who fall and lifts
up all who are bowed down."*

(PSALM 145:14)

In 1992 I met Victor Podluzhny, a former Soviet Naval Officer. Victor had risen to the rank of commander on a submarine with nuclear weapons, and was a hard-nosed atheist with his sights on the ultimate naval prize of becoming an Admiral. One day, patrolling in the Barents Sea, a torpedo supply boat collided with his sub, resulting in the drowning deaths of five sailors in the smaller boat. Although Victor, as he tells it, "had a hundred sailors under my command, with weapons that could destroy entire cities, I could not keep those men from drowning." God used this experience to awaken new sensibilities in Victor's soul. Troubled by the sight of the drowning men, and knowing the incident would stall his rise to the admiralty, he later retired and began life as a civilian.

Still fairly young and needing to maintain an income, Victor began using his car to run a private, taxi-type service, something common at the time in Moscow. This was how we met him, paying for rides across town! He was trying hard to learn English, just as we were trying hard to learn Russian, so we helped each other. In the course of those rides, over time, Victor told us his story, and we told him ours.

The AIA families began inviting him to our homes for dinner, sharing the message of Christ and building trust. Victor also was an accomplished sportsman, excelling in volleyball and having won the national military swimming championship. He respected athletes, and he respected people whose lifestyle lined up with what they claimed to be. He knew about priests who wore robes in monasteries and mechanically observed traditions, but the sight of Olympian sportsmen talking with passion about a relationship with Christ began tugging on his interest. Being in our homes, seeing how our families interacted with love and moral principle centered in the worship of God—all of this began pulling strong on his spirit and mind. One evening, as Ron Nelson shared with Victor, he prayed to receive Christ. By the power of the Gospel, the career communist had become an impassioned believer hungry for the mission field! Victor became a regular with AIA, building great personal and ministry relationships with Steve, Ron, myself and others, and eventually growing into an effective evangelist and our main national administrator for sports ministry in Russia.

Steve Barrett and Victor Podluzhny (key teammates for over 30 years)

Another major development in 1992 was the first AIA sports ministry conference, a three-day event held in Moscow. We were pioneers in international sports ministry, but our goal was to train nationals in each country to eventually take the torch. The Moscow conference was a major step in that direction, with more than 40 Russian-speaking people coming to learn about using sports as a way of sharing the Gospel and worshiping God with the talents He has given. In a nutshell, we told them, "God can use the love you have for sports as a way to bring you closer to Him and to others." Not everyone in attendance was a high-level sportsperson, but everyone there either loved sports or saw it as a way to advance the Gospel. They came away with knowledge, vision, and confidence that they would not be alone in their work of building ministries using sports, but they could count on us and our partnerships to help with training and resources. Over the next two decades, the model of this conference would spread to more than a dozen Republics in the former Soviet Union.

About two months later, Don and Danka Zellmer joined our team in Moscow, right at the time I was heading to Barcelona for my first experience as an official Olympic Chaplain. At most Olympics, the chaplains live outside the Village and commute each day, which complicates access to the athletes. Having credentials to actually live in the Village provided ministry opportunities I had prayed for and dreamed of. Among the Barcelona highlights was a Bible study in which David Robinson, the superstar center for the San Antonio Spurs, brought to the study several of his teammates on the USA Dream Team. But what I enjoyed the most, of course, was access to the wrestlers, many of whom I already knew through competition in international events.

As an Olympic chaplain, my role was not so much evangelistic as to bring presence for spiritual care among athletes already seeking God. The relationships I had built over the years with coaches and athletes were a useful enabler, helping me get personal time with those who were open to sharing their hearts and listening to my message on being a total athlete. What a joy to talk with Olympians about the stronger motivation of offering our training and performances to God, and building our athletic skills on a spiritual foundation through a personal relationship with Jesus Christ.

A turning point on the downside came near the end of the competitions, on the last Sunday. I was scheduled to share God's word in the chapel, and Dr. Bill Bright was coming in to give a greeting. As I walked to the Village security gate to welcome him, the beauty of a Spanish summer morning filled my lungs and my mood. Dr. Bright was the influencer whom God had used in 1976, when I wrote my name in the Soviet Union area on a world map, and now I was greeting him in Spain as an Olympic chaplain based in Moscow! As Dr. Bright came through the gate and we exchanged greetings, his face showed an intensity that seemed out of sync with the festive occasion. Suddenly he said to me, "Carl, Bud is on his deathbed. He's been in an accident and it doesn't look like he will survive."

Wow. Those words hit like punches to the stomach. I literally had to sit down in a chair by the fence. Bud Hinkson was among the very top influencers and mentors in my life, and over the years I had accumulated wonderful memories with him and his family. His wife, Shirley, his son and daughter, John and Joi, were all such special people to Noreen and me and to so many others. The image of Bud on a hospital bed in a comatose state pulled hard on my heart. I do not even remember walking from the gate to the chapel, and for the rest of the day I got through by focusing on what was right in front of me, what I needed to do in the moment.

Life can change so fast. Bud had gone out for a ride on his bicycle and never came back. The Scripture says we are not to *"grieve like the rest of mankind, who have no hope"* (1 Thessalonians 4:13), and I knew Bud would soon be going to his reward, but still I could not shake the numbness.

The Olympics finished, and soon after that I was back in Moscow with sunny Barcelona and the cheerfulness of the Village behind me. In September we moved into the 16th floor of a high rise, with the Barretts living on the 15th floor. Summer was quickly giving way to the far-north weather changes, and by December the daylight hours stretched from 10 in the morning until three in the afternoon. On severely cold days, instead of going outside for exercise, Steve and I would run up the indoor steps five times. Life and ministry went on, and I pushed through with my daily duties, but my family and teammates noticed a difference in my attitude and personality. I started hearing comments such as, "You don't seem like the normal Carl." I was doing a lot more eating, and a lot less praying and Bible reading. My energy level dropped, and my sarcasm level rose. A comment of mine from a prayer letter indicates the mood I struggled with: "The long, dark, cold winters can sometimes be depressing."

The high rise apartment complex in Moscow where the
Dambmans, Barretts, Zellmers and Radunzels lived

For those who have not struggled with depression, it can be a hard experience to describe. What triggers or sustains it can be a mystery, and in this case, the news on Bud was the trigger, but what was already *there* for the triggering? Sometimes, our own experiences can baffle us, along with those whose lives are closely knit to ours. My wife is a Registered Nurse who loves me and understands me, and one day she said, "Carl, I want you to get up at seven o'clock and prepare school lunches for the kids." That was a smart move, because it got me out of bed, even if just to a different room in the apartment.

By the late spring of 1993, I was not wanting to do much of anything, and one day some leaders from Cru met with Noreen and me, suggesting a return to the U.S. for counseling. I knew I could benefit from help, but I saw it as failure and resisted the idea of returning. I managed to push forward as the lead organizer in our annual May conference, and also to maintain the weekly Bible study and fellowship gatherings in our apartment.

Moscow State University behind our AIA conferees during sports activities

During those months, a young Russian named Andrew Lapiga entered our lives at AIA. He had trusted Christ after competing against the Charlotte Eagles and hearing the testimonies of the players, and next thing we knew, he was coming to our weekly Bible studies and bringing one or two of his friends along. When I first met Andrew, seeing him on a field preparing for warmups, I thought he was an American. He wore nice tennis shoes and a sports jacket with some kind of logo, and when I introduced myself, he spoke to me in fluent English with no accent. I soon learned that he came from a successful family and had majored in American dialects at the university. After Andrew came to faith in Christ, we sensed right away he was going to become a key person in ministry among the Russian nationals. Meanwhile, although I was going through the motions of life and ministry, I was really just winging it from day to day. The people who were closest to me, in family and ministry, knew something had to change. Finally, I agreed to a 10-week furlough to the U.S. for counseling sessions twice a week.

During the long flight across the ocean, it seemed like a bad dream. In 1979 I had flown from the U.S. to Europe for a life of mission work, and now, 14 years later, I was flying back for therapy. During those 10 weeks in the States, I did not tell even my key supporters why I was back, or that I had been temporarily removed as team leader. That was a spiritual misstep on my part, since God's word instructs us to share our struggles with one another, so we can pray for one another to experience the power of God's healing available in all areas of our lives (cf. James 5:16). I denied our supporters the opportunity to support me in prayer, and I denied myself the advantage of their support.

During the weeks of counseling, I learned some things about self-talk and focusing on the positive, and I was grateful for a counselor who listened and did his best to point me in the right direction. But, really, my recovery did not pick up steam until I got back to Moscow. The biggest lesson I had needed to learn was to apply more effectively what I already knew. I needed to fix my gaze on God, instead of on my situations, and to remind myself of who I really am in Jesus Christ. It was like Peter walking on the water, and how he started to sink when he shifted his gaze from Christ to his circumstance. Taking our eyes off

Christ can be our tendency, to gaze at the situation and glance at God, when what we need to do is glance at the situation and gaze at God.

Not every Christian has wrestled on a mat in a gym, but every Christian wrestles daily in the battles of spiritual warfare. In these mental and spiritual competitions of daily life, we need to always remember the basics. Like in wrestling, where the fundamentals are things like the stance, with the feet spread right and the hands in front, there are also basics in the spiritual life. This experience after Barcelona showed me the need to always stay conditioned spiritually with the basics.

Back in Moscow, I would go out for walks in the woods that started about 50 yards from our apartment and went on for miles. Something which helped me so much was listening to cassette tapes and reading literature by a Christian psychologist named Dr. Neil T. Anderson. He used the simplicity of Scripture to lay out so plainly, point by point, who we are in Christ, with verses to powerfully back up each point. I was able to zero in on the facts that, in Christ, I am accepted, I am secure, and I am significant. During my walks and throughout each day I would say out loud the truths of God's word that I needed for shaping my mind and heart with God's wisdom.

CHAPTER FOURTEEN
The Gospel and Taekwondo!?!
───

"I have become all things to all people, so that by all possible means I might save some."
(1CORINTHIANS 9:22)

B y the middle of 1994, I was reassigned as team leader and had learned a lot through that humbling experience. That year, St. Petersburg hosted the Goodwill Games, with 2,000 athletes from 56 countries participating in the 16-day event. I had approached the local organizing committee with a proposal for chaplaincy at the Games, and when they agreed, we partnered with a team led by Annette Neely, a sports missionary from Seattle who had moved to St. Petersburg earlier in the decade. Boris Yeltsin opened the Games on July 23. A team of AIA Moscow volunteers, together with the local ministry team, manned an information table with Christian literature in the lobby of the Athlete's Hotel. We also prepared a chapel room where we offered daily Bible studies for the competitors and coaches. Another highlight was having Noreen and the kids join me for the second week of the Games.

Later in that year, I went back to Barcelona for the European Sports Union conference. When I got there, I saw two Christian Taekwondo experts who had developed a way to use their sport for sharing Christ and teaching the Bible. This was amazing to me, because three years earlier the Lord had used me to keep those guys in sports after they came to faith.

This particular story starts in Moscow back in 1991, when Steve Barrett and I attended a seminar in a large auditorium where Bud Hinkson and Ronnie Stevens were two of the main speakers. During the seminar, I was asked to share my testimony of how I used wrestling as a way of worshiping God and as a platform for sharing the Gospel. When I finished, as I was leaving the stage, a tall, athletic-looking guy approached me and said, "My name is Ion. My friend Vasile and I need to talk with you." Ion's voice had a sound of urgency and excitement, so I motioned for Steve Barrett, who was standing nearby, to join us while Ion motioned to Vasile. A few seconds later, the four of us were huddled in an area away from the crowd.

Ion started by briefly sharing his testimony of being a black belt in Taekwondo and a former gang leader in Moldova, "and then I gave up the gang life and street fighting after becoming a Christian." He pointed to his friend and said, "Vasile saw the change in me, and he also became a Christian." We told those guys we were glad to hear this great testimony of how Christ had come into their hearts, and that is when Ion held up his hands and said, "But some of the church leaders are telling us we have to stop practicing Taekwondo." He said something like, "They told us Taekwondo is violent and promotes aggression, and we cannot be Christians and still practice it."

I looked over at Steve, as though to say, "Which one of us wants to go there?" Steve nodded with a smile while pointing to me, which made sense, since those guys had just heard me talk about wrestling and competing internationally while sharing the Gospel. I started by opening a Bible and showing a half-dozen verses that did not line up with what they had been told. I lowered the Bible and looked up to see their eyes glued on mine. They had trained hard for many years to excel in a sport they loved, and I knew they were hungry to learn how they could use Taekwondo in their new lives as Christians. I also knew church traditions are important for keeping order and cultural identity, but everything needs to be tested by the word of God.

I finished by turning to 1 Corinthians 7:20 and reading, *"Each person should remain in the situation they were in when God called them."* I looked at them and said, "Where you were when you trusted Christ, remain there, unless God moves you somewhere else." I explained that for me as a wrestler, my biggest influence was with the wrestlers, a sport I had competed in since age twelve. I said, "That is where people best understand me, where I have trust and relationships." I paused, then added, "Taekwondo is where you guys have influence, where you can draw people and build respect, trust, and relationships."

After the seminar, Ion and Vasile went back to Moldova, and I did not see them again until the Barcelona conference in 1994. In those intervening years, they had developed a way to link the Taekwondo belt-color system to courses in inductive Bible study, connecting each belt to a more advanced level of spiritual knowledge. So, when parents put their kids into one of the clubs, the kids were drawn progressively into the world of the Bible through Taekwondo.

To this day, when people ask me, "What was the most memorable thing God did through you in Russia?", I say it was the half-hour Steve Barrett and I spent with Ion and Vasile. Those guys look back to Steve and me as the ones God used to keep them in sport.

Moldova Taekwondo Team, led by Ion (front-center), with Vasile at far right

Another story from 1994 is worth space in these pages, and it concerns a popular American-style football team called the *Russian Demons*. Backing up again to the high-impact year of 1991, I was able to get the Demons coach to sit down one day and go through a Bible study. He ended up praying to receive Christ, and about four months later, when we met again for study and fellowship, he brought nearly 20 of his players with whom he had been sharing the Gospel! The knowledge of Christ and the Bible had largely been hidden from those men for all of their lives, but they respected their coach, and when he began speaking with them about a personal relationship with Jesus and the value of the Bible, they were willing at least to listen. From there, the Holy Spirit took over, and by February of 1994 the Gospel had so powerfully affected the team that they changed their name to the *Russian Mustangs*. Not long after, when legendary Dallas Cowboy coach Tom Landry came to Moscow with Josh McDowell's ministry outreach, we arranged for Coach Landry to share his testimony with the Mustangs. Those kids loved it, and afterward he showed their team how to run a shotgun offense. It was a great time.

AIA Moscow ministry teammates Don Zellmer, Brian Westfallen, and Steve Barrett, with NFL Hall of Fame Coach Tom Landry (center)

Another year passed, and in the fall of 1995, Barry and Bernice Buehler arrived in Moscow to join us. Our AIA Russia team now consisted of Noreen and me, the Buehlers, the Barretts, and the Podluzhnys. McNick and Andrew were often with us, helping with translation and other areas of ministry, including the Friday night Bible studies in our apartment. In those weekly gatherings, we had a tradition of making submarine sandwiches, slicing up the rolls, then putting out the meat, lettuce, tomatoes, and other fixings. For a group of young guys, that was really something to look forward to, with all of us informally talking about sports, enjoying food, and hearing stories from the Bible. Those Friday night gatherings were a real highlight, starting in the mid-90s and going on for as long as we lived there.

Friday night Bible Study/fellowship in our apartment

Women's weekly Bible Study group in our home. So thankful for Shirley Hinkson (far right) joining to lead the study when she was in Moscow

In 1995 we began expanding the outreach for the annual Moscow sports-ministry conference. The model of our conference gradually spread throughout the former Soviet Union, helping all the more to overcome cultural resistance to the idea of sports ministry, and providing a solid training experience in how to do it. In that same year, we changed the name of the international school to *Hinkson Christian Academy* (HCA), after having opened it to people from other organizations. The school had started with 12 students in 1991, and by the end of the decade we had more than 200. During our first two years, the Moscow Bible Church, the school, and the annual conference were three of the most important developments which continue bearing fruit to the present day.

Another key target in the Moscow region were reform schools and prisons, where we showed films, did wrestling demonstrations, and sometimes split into small groups for discussions about faith. Victor directed that part of our ministry, assisted by a Russian named Eugene, who had been imprisoned as a teenager after being informed on for listening to Christian radio broadcasts in the 1960s. To this day, Eugene continues to serve as a key person for prison ministry in Russia.

By that time, Reid had moved from Czechoslovakia back to Atlanta, where he worked for AIA on Global Sports Events, focusing largely on the upcoming 1996 Olympics. I was invited to serve as a wrestling volunteer, and my son David worked alongside me, helping with translation in both Russian and German. One day the Mongolian wrestling coach was interviewed on local television, and David did the translating, leaving the camera crew and others amazed at seeing the 15-year-old son of American missionaries move so casually back and forth in the languages. What a thrill to have my son working beside me in ministry.

Back in Russia, we got another big boost through Billy Graham's outreach, which really helped in crossing the cultural divide and getting people to open their minds to more exciting ways of thinking about what it means to be a Christian. Steve and I were able to meet Dr. Graham one day at the U.S. ambassador's residence, and his time in Russia softened the ground and helped with new opportunities for the work we were doing.

It was an honor to speak with Dr. Graham and thank him
for his faithful service to the Gospel worldwide

Steve and other Cru staff unload tons of aid at
the airport into trucks for distribution

Another example of partnering with or even riding the coattails
of other ministries was our involvement with Josh McDowell's
humanitarian outreaches, and also with Samaritan's Purse, which for
many years donated thousands of boxes of gift items that we helped

distribute in places like children's hospitals and orphanages. One Christmastime memory which really stands out is driving down a potholed road in a van through the Russian countryside, coming finally to an old brick building surrounded by rolling hills with towering trees. The building housed precious little orphans, as young as six. Together with some members from churches in the region, we unloaded nearly a hundred shoeboxes filled with gifts from American families, along with sports equipment and bulk foodstuffs for the kitchen staff.

The children watched in silent curiosity as we stacked the boxes and then introduced ourselves as Christian friends who had come to share God's love for them. After playing some games in their school courtyard, we gathered them in a big room where they learned a few songs and watched a short video. We explained the real meaning of Christmas, and then we went to the dormitories where we handed out presents. How can I describe the joy of watching little Igor showing me how his matchbox car could fly from his bed to his chair, or looking at little Masha as she tugged on my arm and wanted me to play with her new doll. Leaving the orphanage at day's end was a bittersweet experience, waving good-bye with tears on our faces as we promised to pray for our new little friends whom we knew would never forget us. I believe those moments hold their value in God's eye forever.

CHAPTER FIFTEEN
Our Children Move to the USA

___

"One generation shall praise Your works to another, and shall declare Your mighty acts."
(PSALM 145:4, NASB)

Building into the lives of young people requires a variety of strategies, and one that served our purpose well was to host entire sport teams in the United States. Part of the arrangement we worked out with key persons in the different countries was to first offer to bring in a U.S. team to compete with their athletes. Once they agreed to this, we presented the offer of hosting one of their teams. We would say something like, "If you will host a U.S. team here, we will host one of your teams in the U.S. All you need to do is fly your guys to New York, and we will take care of the rest." From that point, Victor would handle arrangements on the Eurasian side, and Steve and I would get things in order on the American side.

This strategy of doing "sports exchanges" proved to be hugely successful, providing opportunity for young Christian athletes from the west to travel, compete, and share their faith in faraway lands, and then for teams of young athletes from other countries to come and experience a welcoming, positive time in the States. One example which stands out is from 1997, when my son David and I, along with Ken Barr and a few others, went to JFK Airport to welcome a teenage team from the Moscow Sports School. From New York, we drove the team in vans to Philadelphia, where Ken, my old high school coach, had arranged for the kids to be housed in Christian homes. Andrew Lapiga had flown in with them and did much of the translating. Along with arranging wrestling matches in the Philadelphia area, we took the team on site-seeing tours, and one day we drove them to Ocean City, New Jersey, where I had a pastor friend who accompanied us for a day on the beach. The teenagers had a great time walking the boardwalk, sharing a meal with the church, and having the opportunity to see Christian families and joyful worship up close.

With my high school coach Ken Barr (left) and
suburban Philadelphia wrestling coaches

Over the years, we heard many testimonies about how those times in Christian homes were blessed by God, not only for the visiting athletes, but also for the families, who came away with a renewed awareness of the spiritual need and hunger in lands where God's love through Christ was not openly proclaimed. The teenagers ate meals at the families' tables, joined in family prayers and Bible studies, went to church and afterward joined in on the discussions about what had been taught. Bill Shubin helped organize one of the Volleyball tours, hosting some of the team at his home, and making arrangements for the others to stay in nearby homes. Victor helped lead that tour and the athletes attended church and played volleyball on a California beach. A lot of lasting memories and life-changing experiences resulted from those exchanges, which continue to be arranged through AIA staff members such as Victor and Steve.

Back in Moscow, we received another big help when John McIntosh, working with a hockey missionary organization, began partnering with us. One example of John's servant leadership and impact was the two years in which he mentored Yermek, a national karate champion and former hooligan from Kazakhstan, who had come to Moscow for the Bible college. John allowed Yermek to sleep on the couch of his small apartment. After two years at the college, staying with John and doing ministry with us, Yermek went back to Kazakhstan and worked with AIA for several years before becoming a pastor.

The AIA Moscow Team with John McIntosh in Canada sweatshirt

In February of 1998, I served as a chaplain at the Winter Olympics in Nagano, Japan. Although I needed to respect protocol and sensitivity in a multi-faith environment, the position of chaplain gave me incredible access to athletes and officials from so many countries, and my knowledge of German and Russian was a strong enabler. During the welcoming ceremony for the Belarus Delegation, one of the coaches said to me, "You have to meet my Christian skiers." He introduced me to Katya and Irina, both strong believers who invited more than a dozen Russian-speaking athletes from various countries for regular times of Bible study and fellowship.

Belarus Christian cross-country skiers Katya and Irina at the 1998 Nagano Olympics

Japanese journalist interviewing Chaplains Reid Lamphere and Carl "Dumbman"

One day in the chapel, a hockey player named Vencislav Satan came in looking for a Bible! Also, one of the chaplains was Paul Kobylarz from the NHL New Jersey Devils organization. Try to imagine a guy named *Satan* and a chaplain from the *Devils* praying together in the name of Jesus! Also in Nagano, a Japanese newspaper ran an article announcing athletes could come to the Olympic Religious Center for "mental support" from "Chaplain Carl *Dumbman*"! Of course, I laughed it off, and we left Nagano with great memories of sharing the faith and enjoying the competitions.

Also in 1998, David graduated from HCA and moved to the Pacific Northwest. We felt proud of the tremendous education David had obtained, and how he managed the challenges of growing up as a son of missionaries in three different countries. From Austria to Germany to Russia, in each new place, as with Stephen and Elisabeth, David had to learn the cultural subtleties and build new friendships. He was 10 when we moved to Moscow, and he felt the hurt of leaving behind his close friendships from our six years in Hallbergmoos. In Moscow, our kids lived through the 1991 coup centered about 20 miles from our apartment, they saw poverty, scarcity, dead bodies of suicide victims, and drunks whom we stopped to drag off icy roads and snowbanks. But in all of that, they grew up surrounded by God's love through their family, church, school, and the extended families of Cru. The friendships our kids developed with other children of missionaries really deepened their dependence on God and their understanding of relationships.

The following year, Elisabeth also graduated and moved to the U.S., where she attended a local community college in Auburn with David. In the summer of 1999, we took a six-month leave and used most of that time for building a house on the five acres Noreen's parents had given us. It was quite a family effort, with Noreen's brothers coming from Utah and Georgia to help clear the land, lay the foundation, put in water and electrical lines, cut and fit the timber, and do the many other chores needed for building a complete house from scratch. Special thanks to David, Stephen, and our nephew Nathan, who at their young ages did the lion's share of the work. Elisabeth spent a lot of overtime in the kitchen, and Noreen helped wherever she was needed. I was the chief gofer, driving my brother-in-law's pickup truck for runs to hardware stores and the lumber yard. A lot of very hard work, but what an incredible time we had together as family. When it was finally done, David and Elisabeth stayed to live in the new house, while Stephen returned with us to finish his education at HCA.

Construction continues as we stand in the front yard.
Left to right Elisabeth, Carl, Noreen, David and Stephen.
Special thanks to our relatives who helped us

Back in Moscow, Rodger Oswald of *Church Sports International* led a seminar aimed to get church leaders more interested and informed on sports ministry. Over a hundred youth ministry leaders, pastors, and church lay people showed very positive responses. They learned how sports ministry is effective for building friendships and fellowship, for evangelism and discipleship, and for integrating people into local churches. During the seminar I met a young Christian volleyball player and college student named Yury Gromyko who had begun using his sport to gather youth in his neighborhood, thinking he had invented sports ministry! When he saw what God had been doing through us, and how many others were already involved, he was amazed. After graduating with a degree in nuclear physics, he joined AIA, and to this day remains one of our key leaders across Eurasia in training others for sports ministry and church planting.

Moscow Leaders gathered after finishing the church
sports conference with guest speakers

With other AIA pioneers, Larry Amundson, John Peterson and Gene Davis,
meeting in Turkey for the Wrestling World Championships in 1999

The Lord blessed the decade to close out with a really memorable experience at the World Wrestling Championships in Turkey, with AIA legends Larry Amundson, Gene Davis, and my old friend, John Peterson. That was October of 1999. A quarter-century had passed since "that hippy from UMass" came lumbering into their retreat in State College, Pennsylvania, and I had lasted more than a month.

A week after leaving Turkey, I was with a USA basketball team in Kazakhstan, on a tour organized annually by Jason Taylor, an AIA staff member living in Central Asia. Starting in 1995, that particular tournament had given a great platform for the Gospel. Jason introduced me to Rashid, whom I mentioned in the Prologue. Rashid was a former Muslim with a mafia-type background, whose heart and life had been transformed by the Gospel. He was part of the Uzbekistan Basketball Federation, where he played and coached. He and I began building a friendship which strengthened our trust for partnering in ministry. He brought his family to Moscow for two years where he attended the Bible college and built lasting relationships with others on the AIA team, especially with Steve Barrett. After returning to Central Asia, Rashid became a strong asset to western missionaries who were striving to learn the language and culture. The guys soon began calling him their "secret weapon," and to this day Rashid is one of our top ministry leaders in Eurasia. There are so many branches of these stories about God bringing people together and doing incredible things to carry forward the Great Commission.

In 2001, Stephen graduated from HCA and moved to Washington. As with his brother and sister, leaving Moscow was difficult because of the deep friendships he had built. Those kids had really been in the foxholes together, especially in Moscow where racial prejudice could at times be strong, and our children were close with those of missionaries from Asian and African countries. Over the years, there were more than just a couple encounters on the streets, where the missionary kids of color were harassed or

AIA Basketball played a great role in the former Soviet Union, with the Gospel shared at each game

attacked, and our children stood with them (or ran off with them!). On one occasion, when Stephen was eleven, a group of Russian boys, one armed with a knife, confronted him. Stephen spotted a grandmother at a kiosk on a sidewalk. Knowing how grandmothers carry weight in Russian culture, he ran up to her and told her what was happening. Sure enough, the elderly woman shooed off the little gang and walked Stephen away.

With the last of our children having gone to the States, Noreen and I had to make an emotional adjustment. After two decades with our children's wonderful presence in foreign lands, and having watched them leave one by one, we really did miss our kids.

By the middle of 2001, we were passing the baton to nationals whom we had helped train. What a blessing to see how Christ had used us to bring in those young people, build them up in their faith and understanding of the Word, and then watch them go out to do the same with others in their home nations and communities. In a nutshell, this captures our approach in AIA sports ministry: Bring them in, build them up, send them out.

The Bible says we are *"Christ's ambassadors"* and *"co-workers in God's service"* (2 Corinthians 5:20; 1 Corinthians 3:9). This identity and this responsibility applies to all Christians, not just to an elite. My book has centered on the story of God's use of athletes to open doors and provide all things for evangelizing and discipling, getting us into countries once considered "closed", and enabling us to build sports ministries and teach others how to do the same. Yet the message of the book is not just about what God can do through athletes, but what He can do through you.

None of us can rightly claim competence for ourselves in the work of ministry, and even the apostle Paul said, *"Not that we are competent in ourselves to claim anything for ourselves, but our competence comes from God"* (2 Corinthians 3:5), and, *"it is God who is at work in you, both to desire and to work for His good pleasure"* (Philippians 2:13). Since it is God who works in us and promises to provide all that is needed for the labor He has chosen, no one has an excuse.

In July of 2001, I flew to South Africa at the invitation of Cassie Carstens, founder of an annual, 12-week Global Sports Ministry School.

I went there to provide three days of instruction on discipleship and the steps for building a national sports ministry, and what I saw amazed me. About two dozen young Christian sports leaders from nearly 20 different countries had come by invitation for intensive training with practical, hands-on experience. Yermek, the Karate Kid, and Katya, the skier I met at Nagano, were there as students. At the school, the students learned to understand the Bible as the foundation for their thinking about themselves, and about everything else. But they gained much more than just head knowledge of the Bible. Their hearts and lives were turned inside out in a cross-cultural environment under experienced coaches and teachers, where they learned not only the mechanics for building sports ministries in their home countries, but also how to build personally into the lives of others.

The school was held on a river island where the water flowed through a canyon with mountains and vineyards on both sides, and the school grounds had a large grassy field surrounded by clusters of trees and a small building with dormitories, offices, and a cafeteria. The students learned servant leadership, the value of team, the value of the Bible and of prayer for life and ministry, all with an end-goal of multiplying disciples. One of the important positions at the school was shepherd (chaplain), filled by a former cricket superstar named Trevor Goddard. Trevor led devotions in the mornings and spent one-on-one time with students, bringing a strong fatherly presence to supplement what the young adults were learning about ministry, faith, and how to coach life skills along with athletic skills in all kinds of different sports. Little did I know that over the next two decades, both Noreen and I would commit a major time investment to the school and its students.

Meanwhile, I was asked to be part of a team overseeing development of sports games for the community in Eurasia, mainly in creative access

With international sports leaders
Cassie and Bassem in South Africa

countries. With Ion from Moldova, and teammates in Poland and Ukraine, we were tasked with creating outreach through sports games for children, teenagers, and families. These various levels of organized games drew many into situations where they heard personal testimonies and short presentations of the Gospel. Although I was the team leader for AIA-Russia, more and more I was focused on global events and in training others how to do chaplaincy, relying on Victor and the team of nationals to keep things going in Moscow.

In December of 2001, Steve and I traveled to Yakutia in Siberia for the Hapsagay Tournament, where we wrestled in the "Veterans" competitions. This was my first competitive match in more than 10 years, and although my physical conditioning was well below par, I came away with a bronze and received the ruble-equivalent of 35 dollars, the most I had ever won in my career! Steve was awarded 100 dollars for winning the silver in his weight class, so, with all expenses covered by those who had invited us, we went home with more cash than we had come with! The people in Yakutia are steeped in traditions of shamanistic culture, but we lovingly shared with them the message of one God and His Son Jesus the Savior, leaving behind literature and praying for Christ to build up the local believers in their faith.

In May of 2002, some tension had developed within our Russia team over whether or not a certain member should be asked to leave the team. This can happen in ministry, with strong differences of opinion among members, threatening the unity of the team in general. As the leader, I had to do what I believed was best, but Victor and Steve disagreed with me. The situation came to a head at a meeting with the Cru national leader on a day which happened to be Noreen and my 25-year wedding anniversary. The outcome of the meeting was not only the removal of the controversial member, but also my removal as team leader. That one really hurt. After the meeting, I went to HCA and met Noreen coming out of the classroom where she taught Health. From there, we went to the room we had reserved at the Hotel Russia on Red Square, where I spent most of the night crying. What a memory from our quarter-century anniversary!

If a person has not been knocked down in mission work or ministry, that person has probably not been around very long. As in athletics, so also in life, every struggle is experience for the journey. Even disappointments are an important part of our long wrestle for victory, and our stumbles can remind us to find our identity and worth in Christ, not in the results of a situation. Today, as I am telling this story in the year 2021, I work with Reid on the Global Events Team for Athletes in Action, meeting frequently on Zoom with Steve, Victor, Rashid, Yury and others concerning AIA-Russia issues. But on that night in 2002, I was only feeling the agony of defeat.

Two months later, we were in Washington, where Noreen's dad was struggling with late-stage cancer. Almost a quarter-century earlier he had run half a mile on the morning of the fire, a man who feared God, loved and served others, and had built up his eighty acres with grit and ingenuity—it was tough, all those years later, to see him fading. Her dad had become a believer in his 30s. With no formal seminary training, after some years in the faith he became the pastor of a small church, while also running a two-man sawmill and providing a strong example as a husband, father and neighbor. Finally, the day came, and her father left the earth surrounded by family, some of whom had come from different states. Noreen was grateful to have been there, helping with the care and with the mutual comforting among loved ones in a difficult time.

Bruised up but pushing on, I launched into our team's next major project of putting together a Sports Bible. This idea had been in the works for a while, but we had only recently come up with the financing. The plan was to use the New International Version of the New Testament in Russian, interspersing it with testimonies and color pictures of Christian athletes well-known in their particular sports. We did this in partnership with other ministries, but Victor and I were given the job of making sure it all came together. Andrew Lapiga helped us, along with Randy Cox, a hockey guy who later went on to become a regional director for Samaritan's Purse.

Doing the Sports Bible took a lot of faith, endurance, and teamwork, spending long days and short nights getting the translation right, getting the font right, meeting deadlines and staying on top of all that was involved. My testimony was in there, along with those of Steve, Victor, John Peterson, and the Taekwondo guys. The end result was, by the grace of God, the Sports Bible was printed and widely distributed, along with a series of twenty-minute evangelistic sports videos in basketball, soccer, and wrestling. One time at an international tennis tournament in Moscow, Andrew Lapiga and I gave out many copies of the Sports Bible, and I was able to personally hand one to Boris Yeltsin. President Yeltsin politely thanked me, then handed the Bible to his nearest bodyguard.

Steve and Carl, excited to share the Russian Sports New Testament, "Path to Victory," at one of our conferences

Another year passed, and in 2004 a spokesperson for a partnership of sports-ministry organizations asked me to oversee the work of putting together a shortened version of the global school. I had been very much involved with that network of organizations since the

1980s, beginning with the huge Congress at the Seoul Olympics and the subsequent Arena Conference in Austria. We all agreed to make it a one week sports ministry training, packing together components of the three-month school. Victor Podluhzny did a great job as my right-hand guy, handling the complex administrative issues, and we held the training at a conference site near Moscow. About 35 leaders in Eurasian sports ministry came for training in using sports as a way of honoring God and accelerating ministry. Cassie Carstens was one of the main teachers, and we all had a great time of fellowship, worship, playing competitive games, and most of all focusing on the use of sports for evangelism and discipleship. This sports ministry training was another big step in preparing nationals to take the torch and carry on, building and growing sports ministries in their home countries and local communities. The model spread throughout Eurasia and beyond, until by the end of the decade, many thousands had gone through the same training.

Sports ministry training led by Cassie, near Moscow with
Yury and Victor and leaders from across Eurasia

CHAPTER SIXTEEN
Major Changes

"There is a time for everything, and a season for every activity under heaven."
(ECCLESIASTES 3:1)

In February of 2005 I received an unexpected call from my brother Bob in Philadelphia. All I remember from the conversation are three words: "Dad is gone." I literally fell to my knees, clutching the receiver somewhere near to my ear, but looking up and crying out in my soul. Within an hour, Noreen and I had arranged for a flight to Philadelphia, where we spent two weeks packing Dad's things. Mom was having a difficult time, losing her husband of 62 years, but she was greatly helped from being surrounded by her children. Although the loss of loved ones has been a part of life since the days of Abel, it hits like a shot to the deepest parts. As far back as my memories can go, my dad is there, standing strong and reaching out with a caring hand. Then, one day, he is gone. Through all of the sorrow, I kept an attitude of gratefulness to God for having given me such a wonderful dad.

Near the end of the month, we returned to Moscow, where life and ministry went on, and the calendar pages kept turning. In 2007, Steve and Cindi Barrett returned to the U.S. for a time, before moving on to Mongolia. We missed them, both as teammates and as friends, but we were grateful for the team now in place. With Victor, Yury, and experienced volunteers, I felt comfortable, even as the team leader, with the frequent traveling I was doing on international ministry commitments.

The annual AIA Russia conference grew to around
150 sports ministry leaders each spring

Later in the year, I was asked to serve as one of the emcees at a global congress on sports, held in Thailand in preparation for the 2008 Olympics in Beijing. About 600 people came from around the world, with Andy Lim, a Chinese friend who grew up in Singapore, serving as the other emcee. Cassie was there, and one day he told me the elderly Trevor was struggling with the physical requirements of the work. He asked if Noreen and I would come to South Africa in 2008, to see if I might be a good fit to carry on the work as shepherd. I told Cassie we would be honored, but we would miss the first two weeks because of my commitment to the Olympic Project in Beijing that summer.

In July of 2008, I flew to Beijing where I worked with over 100 AIA participants in the outreaches. Each morning, we all gathered for prayer, Bible reading, praise and fellowship, before heading out to the Olympic Venues. One of the side-highlights from my time in China was going for a hike with the U.S. Freestyle Wrestling Team and Bill Shubin on the Great Wall. How amazing to take in the view, and to think of all the history that Wall has seen.

From Beijing, I made a stop in Seattle where Noreen was waiting, and with her I flew on the red eye to South Africa. After more than 24 hours on airplanes and at airports, we grabbed a night of rest and then got busy building into the lives of the students. Each morning at 7:00 we had devotions, and throughout the days I looked for any way I could bring presence to build trust and openness. As the weeks passed, I saw how God was blessing me with deep and meaningful relationships among many of the students. One day, as I was taking it all in, what God had done in my life since meeting Noreen and joining AIA, the amazement of His faithfulness and mercy overwhelmed me, and the tears started rolling down my face.

During those weeks in South Africa, the Lord blessed Noreen to become a Mom-figure among the students, and when the three-month training had ended, Cassie asked us to come back the following year. Little did my wife and I know that we would become long-term members of the school's international team which included local staff, prayer partners, and teachers and facilitators brought in from around the world. For each of the next 11 years, we would spend on average about 10 weeks with the team in South Africa.

The next big development came in 2009, with the opening of a four-week training school in Ukraine. A lot of work went into getting started, with a Ukrainian friend named Igor and his basketball-coach wife, Iryna, both graduates of the South African school, driving around with me and knocking on doors, until finally Christ opened what no one could shut. The idea was to provide more extensive preparation for nationals than a local training program, without requiring the three-month time-investment and English-knowledge requirement of the global training. Working in partnership with a coalition of Russian-speaking ministries, in June, we started the *Eurasian Sports Ministry School,* with Yury Gromyko as the director. One year later, in Germany, our partners did the same in a city near Frankfurt, starting the *European Sports Ministry School.* Getting those four-week schools up and running are among the best experiences I can remember in ministry teamwork.

Taekwondo Master Ion teaching Inductive Bible Study
Method at Eurasian Sports Ministry School near Kyiv

In the same year we got hit with a huge loss. Noreen's mom, Norma, went to be with the Lord at the age of 80. She had struggled with cancer for about a year, so we knew the day was coming, but there is no way to fully prepare for losing someone so special. One of Norma's most wonderful gifts was the way she listened to people and went deep in her relationships. I will never forget her holding baby Elisabeth in our apartment in Vienna, and so many other wonderful memories of my dear mother-in-law. One of her most outstanding virtues was how she rarely if ever had anything negative to say about anyone. Such a kind-hearted, modest, responsible, and encouraging woman who would not hesitate to make sacrifices for others. Noreen was so thankful to be there for the last month, sad of course, but grateful to our God for having been given a mother who so deeply loved and cared for her family. The Lord arranged that she could be with both her mom and dad as they passed through the shadow of death.

By 2010, my international commitments had expanded to include the Summer and Winter Olympics, the World University Games (held each odd-numbered year between the Olympics), the International Wrestling Championships (serving the USA team), and the biggest time commitment of all, my shepherding role at the school in Africa. This meant I was spending time outside of Russia for about six months each year, while also serving as team leader for AIA-Russia. The guys back in Moscow were highly capable, worked together as a team, and had been trained well, but the Cru/AIA leadership began suggesting I should spend more time focusing locally. They had their good reasons, and I respected them. But I also had my good reasons, and I did not want to pull back on my commitments to people in faraway places who had worked so hard to build their ministries. A friend of mine described the emerging challenge as a tension between "organizational need and personal calling."

To be effective in ministry commitments, I needed to bring presence, and for that I needed sufficient time-investments in different places around the world. I knew the leadership was wanting a decision from me, to either focus more on Moscow, or close out my position as team leader. Since I had confidence my team in Russia could do just fine during my frequent absences, I decided to continue with what I had been doing, and to see what came next.

Well, what came next was different than what anyone had expected. After being in Siberia in January with the USA wrestling team, then in Vancouver as a chaplain at the 2010 Winter Olympics (where my teammate DJ and I marched in with the Belarus delegation for closing ceremonies), Noreen and I visited family in Auburn. Two days later, we boarded a plane destined for Moscow where I planned to help the USA Wrestling Team at the World Cup. Shortly after takeoff from Seattle, I began having chest pains. When I could no longer stand it, I stood up and signaled for the flight attendants. It "just so happened" that a doctor was on the plane, and he gave instructions for the attendants to give me nitro and oxygen, while also advising an emergency landing. A short while later, we touched down in Minneapolis, where I was rushed by ambulance to United Hospital in St. Paul. After 24 hours in ICU, the doctors ruled out a cardiac issue, and diagnosed a gall stone that was blocking a duct. Three days after they removed the stone, Tom Lamphere, still in Minneapolis as chaplain for the Vikings, brought me some clean underwear from Walmart, and Noreen and I flew back to Seattle. DJ sent a hilarious email, giving his theory for why I had gotten sick: "Maybe too much McDonald's at the Olympics!" It is great to have friends unafraid to lighten up a situation with a joke.

In April, on my 60th birthday, I was at AIA headquarters in Ohio. One day I was asked to attend a small meeting where the leaders told me, "Carl, we really think you need to move back to the U.S. We need to look at what kind of position is right for you, and we want you to move to Ohio." I had been with AIA for 35 years, and hearing those words from the leadership felt like punches to the gut. No final decision was made on that day, but it was clear something would need to give soon.

Shortly after leaving the room and praying tearfully with a friend named Brad, I got an email from my son David, saying, "I am so proud that you are my father. I respect you so much. I am grateful for the man of God you are, how you love Mom and each of us kids, and the role model you have been in my life. Happy Birthday. I love you, Dad." I stared at the email, re-reading it for the words to really sink in. Just a few hours earlier, I had been told after 20 years in Russia, not everyone was happy with my work there. That blow had brought me to tears, but the loving words of respect and gratefulness from my son worked as a counterweight. I thanked God for His hand upon me for good.

After leaving Ohio, I flew back to our home in Auburn before returning to Moscow. One day I went walking with our dog, Polo, down the gravel road, listening to the Bible on a Walkman. As we came to the creek that runs through the family property, I listened to the story about Abraham being told to sacrifice his firstborn son (Genesis chapter 22). As I was thinking through the story, I stopped and hit the pause button. Right there by the creek, I understood God was telling me to sacrifice everything to Him, including my dreams of mission work centered in Russia. I turned off the tape and went into prayer, offering it all to God through Christ, and I walked away feeling the Lord had taken some of the weight off my shoulders. When I got home and talked about this with Noreen, she expressed she was ready to live back in the States and be near our family.

The day of decision came in February of 2011, just before the start of the Winter Asian Games in Kazakhstan, where a friend named Pavel had offered to let me sleep on his couch for 10 days while I participated in various outreaches at the multi-sport competitions. Before going to Kazakhstan, I flew to Slovenia for a Cru conference. On the last day in Slovenia, I met with some of the leaders, who told me, "Carl, we really need you in Moscow nine months a year." I paused for a moment, then leaned forward in my chair and said, "How about six months?" The regional director slightly shook his head and said, "No, it is either nine months, or you need to report back to the States." I had hoped for some compromise, so I did feel disappointment, but I also understood those in leadership were wanting team leaders around the world to spend more time focusing locally while turning the ministries over to nationals. Also, I knew God was directing the course of things, and we would end up wherever He was leading.

I left the meeting knowing our time of living in Moscow was over. God had blessed me with wonderful team members, had enabled my children to safely negotiate their years of growing up in a big, bustling city, had walked me through hard experiences, and had caused our work in Moscow to bear ongoing fruit. The thought of walking away from all of that was tough, but I knew the nationals would continue doing a great job.

No decision had been made on just what I would be doing for AIA back in the States, and I was not even sure I would be staying with the organization. The one sure thing I knew was that the time had come for Noreen and me to leave Russia. Moscow had been our home for two decades, but God was bringing us to a new phase.

Shortly after the meeting, I flew to Kazakhstan, where I expected to see Pavel at the airport. We landed at four in the morning, and as I crossed the tarmac toward the gate, I saw a guy holding a large sign with my name on it. That was strange. I approached the person and said, "I am Carl Dambman." He nodded and said, "Just follow me." I held up my hand and said, "I think somebody is meeting me at another gate." He said, "No, the Kazakhstan Olympic Committee sent me here to meet you." Over the years and decades, I had built up a good relationship with that committee, but I had no idea what this was about. I followed the guy as he escorted me to the VIP lounge, and from there I was driven to the Intercontinental Hotel in downtown Almaty, which I knew would cost several hundred dollars a night. I told him, "I cannot pay this much for a room, and it was already arranged for me to sleep on somebody's couch." He gave a friendly laugh and assured me I would not be sleeping on a couch during my time in his country.

What ended up happening is that I not only stayed for 10 days in a luxurious hotel room, but was taken each day in a limo from the hotel to the Games, with a police escort! The Kazakhstan Olympic Committee explained to me that because I had helped them so much in places like Nagano and Vancouver, they wanted to express their gratitude. Well, I was not going to turn that down! During my 10 days there, the Olympic Committee paid all costs for me to have an assigned driver, eat free meals, sleep in a five-star hotel, have a Kazak translator, and have credentials that would get me into any event I wanted to see. It was a great combination of being able to do ministry with the local sports guys, and to also enjoy the Games. Coming just a week after the painful experience in Slovenia, I saw this as God assuring me He was still in control, and He was always working *"to do immeasurably more than all we ask or imagine"* (Ephesians 3:20).

Chaplains Dave Johns, Katya, Carl, and Paul
Kobylarz at 2010 Vancouver Olympics

Carl with Pavel's family and sports ministry
friends at the ski jump in Almaty, 2011

CHAPTER SEVENTEEN
Back in the USA

—

"And even when I am old and gray, O God, do not forsake me, until I declare Your strength to this generation, Your power to all who are to come."
(PSALM 71:18)

I n May of 2011, Noreen and I flew back to the States, to start the post-Moscow years of our life together. We had much to reflect on since the flight out of JFK in 1979, and I think we both felt the amazement of looking back on how God had shown His loving faithfulness in so many ways during our decades overseas. Always in life, we look back on the years and see the things we would like to have done differently. One example for me were the times when Noreen had expressed how she would like me to be at home more. I was grateful for a wife who was understanding and had the same values, but there were times I felt the tension between being away in ministry and spending more time at home. I knew, in times to come, when mentoring ministry workers who are fathers of young families, I would caution them against sacrificing their families on the altar of ministry. For Christian men, it is so important to remember our mission for Christ begins in our homes.

After settling in at our house in Washington, the big question was where I would now fit in with AIA? The leadership offered several possibilities, but most involved being in Ohio in an office. One day I said to Noreen, "Honey, I am not an office guy, I am a field guy. I like to be out meeting people, sharing my faith, doing activities and hosting events." She already knew this, of course, and she supported my decision to not accept an office role in the AIA structure. There had to be something which my gifting from God, and my lifetime of experience, better suited me for. I suggested to the leaders that they let me work with Reid, somebody who knew my strengths and weaknesses, who valued me and wanted me as part of his team. They agreed, and one day I got a call from Ohio saying, "Carl, you live near Seattle, Reid lives near Atlanta, but you guys have a good relationship, you both love to travel, so you are going to be part of the Global Events Team of Athletes in Action."

I called Reid, and we got started. My first big assignment was the 2012 Summer Olympics in London, where I served as an international chaplain. This was a great experience, and the year was going well until one day I got a call from Yury about Kostya Molov, one of our key guys among the next generation to whom we were passing the baton. His wife was Lana, whose heart also was committed to mission work. Kostya had just finished training a group of pastors on sports ministry, and while I was out in the yard at home, when the call came in from Yury, I expected a great report on how things had gone. Yury said, "Carl, terrible news. Kostya and Lana were killed in a car crash." I felt numb, trying to get my head around what I had just heard. Kostya was among the most faithful and reliable missionary workers I had ever known, and we had worked so hard to build into him our knowledge and experience. Why?

As humans, we look at things and try to put together a structure, but an experience like that is hard to fit into a pattern. I thought of the pain of Kostya's family, especially his sister Katya, who is also one of our key people in that part of the world. Over the next few days, I drew heavily from the story of Jesus when He said:

"Very truly I tell you, unless a kernel of wheat falls to the ground and dies, it remains only a single seed. But if it dies, it produces many seeds." (John 12:24; cf. Luke 8:8)

Somehow, in the mystery of God's working, what happened with Kostya and Lana had a purpose in the Great Commission of Christ in building His church. We see life from inside the story we are living, and from this standpoint, life does not always make sense or fit into a pattern. A big part of what it means to be a Christian in the Biblical sense is to not question God's ways, but to obey His command to love and to make disciples. The Bible tells us plainly:

"The secret things belong to the Lord our God, but the things revealed belong to us." (Deuteronomy 29:29)

"Let us hear the conclusion of the whole matter: Fear God and keep His commandments: for this is the whole duty of man." (Ecclesiastes 12:13, KJV)

The Bible does not answer every question of human curiosity, but it gives us all we need for learning how to win the imperishable prize of pleasing God.

"Let no wise man boast of his wisdom...but let the one who boasts boast of this: that he understands and knows Me, that I am the Lord." (Jeremiah 9:23-24, NASB)

Bruised up once again, we all continued to push. Those whom Kostya and Lana had mentored in Russia carried the torch, such as Ivan in Moscow and Alexander in Volgograd, and so many others. Meanwhile, in the summer of 2013, the World University Games were in Kazan, Russia, where I served as an official chaplain among more than 10,000 athletes. In the winter of 2014, the Olympics were in Sochi, where I served again as a chaplain. This was also the year of the challenging experience in Tashkent, as related in the Prologue.

In April of 2015, Noreen and I spent three weeks at the Gold Camp in Myanmar (Burma), where the country's elite athletes were trained. We had been invited by the Minister of Sports and Tourism to help their country's athletes prepare for the Southeast-Asian Games, and part of my job was to teach with DJ on team-conflict management and the fear of failure in sports. Reid and Carolyn were also there. Since we were in a secular environment, we needed to be careful with how we worded our presentations of Biblical principles, and we were challenged by a woman who had some kind of authority and influence, even over the director.

The woman did what she could to sabotage our access and our project, and even tried getting us kicked out of the country on the charge of being "missionaries." She started out very confident in what she could do, not realizing she was up against experienced veterans in creative ministry. Our experience over decades had taught us to be fast on our feet and always confident through Christ that a way would open for testimony and discipleship. Our time in Gold Camp showed once again the faithfulness of Christ and His power available to all who step out of the boat to come to Him. The Lord Jesus would not have sent us out if He were not going to open the doors. We cannot rightly say ANY country is "closed to the Gospel," because Christ will always provide a way in, and one of those ways is sports.

In July, I was in South Korea for the World University Games, then off to South Africa with Noreen for the School. In September, I flew to Las Vegas for the World Wrestling Championships, where we were working to set up an official chaplaincy program. In November, I was in Orlando with over 650 sports ministry leaders from around the world, gathered for the annual global sports ministry evaluation and planning meetings. This is where we launched a sports-ministry resource program called *ReadySetGO.world*. A couple weeks later I was in Turkey with more than 250 leaders from the Eurasia sport ministry teams, encouraging the younger leaders to take the ministry to the next level.

On the last day of that busy year, I got a call from my brother Bob, informing me our mom was not going to last more than a few days. Within hours, I had boarded a plane from Seattle to Philadelphia, hoping to get there in time to say good-bye. When I landed, Bob met me at the airport and said, "Carl, Mom is gone." He and his wife Jayne had been with her when she passed in the early hours of New Year's Day. I felt the disappointment, but my comfort was the confidence that she was with Dad in the presence of our Lord. Over the next few days, I was joined by my brothers and sister as we packed up Mom's belongings and made arrangements for the memorial service. The Bible says, *"One generation commends Your works to another; they tell of Your mighty acts"* (Psalm 145:4). My mother had done a great job raising four children and being a volunteer in the community, and I could write an entire book talking about her and my dad.

Later in 2016, Noreen and I flew from South Africa to Rio, where I served as one of the international chaplains at the Summer Olympics.

Carl at center in back row (with blue ski hat), ready to march in at the Opening Ceremonies as part of the USA Delegation at the Winter University Games in Almaty, Kazakhstan

Also in 2017, AIA celebrated 50 years at the Ohio headquarters.
AIA wrestlers were honored (left to right: Carl, Gene Davis,
Larry Amundson, John Klein, John Peterson, and Reid)

In 2017, I was back in Kazakhstan for ten days at the Winter World University Games, having the role of transportation coordinator with the U.S. delegation. Eating three meals a day in the Athletes Village cafeteria gave me opportunities to connect informally with many of the USA athletes and others.

Then, in 2018 I was back in Korea, where the Belarussian Olympic Committee gave me and an AIA teammate day passes for access to the Village. This was my seventh time at the Winter Olympics, and my 18th Olympic experience overall.

In 2019, the last year before the pandemic, I made three trips to Russia, including one for our 28th sports leadership conference in Moscow. Bill Shubin accompanied us and continued his long-term support of AIA missionaries and their work. Soon after, it was off to Peru with Reid and the Global Events Team for the Pan American Games. Also in 2019, a bunch of us got an email from Don Zellmer, relating a message he had received from AIA volunteers in Ukraine: "Come over and help us!" A short time later, Don was heading off to

Kyiv, just as he had gone off to Vienna four decades earlier. He ended his email by saying, "My good buddy John Peterson will join us over there." Wow. More than 40 years had passed since we all flew together to Iran and Bulgaria, and the old guys are still marching.

Another beautiful example is Steve Barrett's ongoing work in Eurasia and Mongolia. Steve's model of camp/tournament has inspired Christian sports leaders to begin holding annual evangelistic sports camps, and the presence of teams of U.S. wrestlers gathered by AIA, partnering with FCA, has helped to establish an atmosphere of love and friendship for facilitating the spread of the Gospel and training as a total athlete.

Year after year, the pace did not slow upon our return to the U.S. From Latin America to South Africa, from Europe to Central Asia and Siberia, we carried on and pushed forward. Each continent now has a group of partners working together to grow the sports ministries that God blessed us to help pioneer in the 70s, 80s, and 90s. Now, the younger generation is taking charge, and they have the generation after them. What a privilege to be a part of the Great Commission, not just "*in Judea and Samaria*" but "*to the ends of the earth*" (Acts 1:8).

The mission, the vision, and the values of AIA have not changed. The ministry has always been to develop influencers in sport, to maximize their impact in evangelism and discipleship. God continues to multiply the workers and send them into the harvest field. From my home near Seattle, I utilize venues such as Zoom, Skype, Telegram and WhatsApp, along with Facebook. Each of these provides an avenue for connecting with people and also enabling me to continue providing mentorship.

Prior to 2020 I was challenged with jet lag, but now it is Zoom fatigue. I am often on calls with key leaders from across Eurasia, with all of us talking in Russian. I get so excited, hearing the training which the nationals are doing in helping people, and talking of the next steps after the pandemic. At the time of this writing, in many places across the world, face-to-face sports ministry (as opposed to Zoom meetings!) is starting to open up. John Peterson and Steve Barrett recently returned from Moldova and Ukraine, where they continued their ministry at wrestling camps.

I get inspired by those who have taken the torch, like the young guys in Eurasia, Singapore, and Canada, who are spearheading a strategy to reach everyone digitally. We miss the old ways, because that is what we knew, but the uncertainty of the future is spiritual opportunity.

Our ways of doing things will be different, but the vision is the same. The heart of sports ministry remains using the platform of athletics to reach others with God's love, and helping athletes and coaches grow in their relationship with Jesus Christ. We need to listen, pay attention to how the world is changing, stay focused on our vision, and seek from God the understanding for how to move forward effectively. After all has been said and done, life for us is still about the Great Commandment and the Great Commission.

AFTERWORD
2021 Tokyo Olympics

Over the past decade, international chaplains have gradually increased their use of new technologies for bringing presence at sporting events. Early in the year 2020, under the restrictions of the pandemic, our Global Events Team began realizing how much training and encouragement we could provide through these avenues. Although face-to-face ministry is our preference, we want to do all we possibly can, and the technologies provide many options for athletes to connect with mentors, disciplers, and prayer partners from far away.

So, although chaplaincy work online was not an entirely new thing, gathering athletes together in a group online is fairly new, and in Tokyo, everything had to be done virtually. Our goal for the Tokyo Olympics was to develop an online Global Athletes Community, connecting athletes who want to grow in their faith and to worship God through sport. We were able to provide, via Zoom, a daily, thirty-minute chapel service, consisting of two worship songs, a Bible verse of the day, a devotional talk, and prayer time. Having served in the Olympic Village during past Games, it was not a matter of athletes just "showing up," as we often had to go out and encourage them to come. Without us physically there, the turnout was sometimes disappointing. Yes, we had hoped for more participation in the chaplaincy services we worked so hard to offer online, but we made the commitment to be there every day for the athletes, whether they showed up or not.

Even with limited participation from the athletes, the highlight for me was seeing our younger AIA staff from Latin America, Africa, Europe, and Asia bringing a strong presence. They served as emcees, giving inspirational and devotional talks, and shared about their lives, in sport and beyond. Our Global Events Team cannot be at every major sports competition, but we can encourage and empower the younger staff to take the lead at regional and world sports events.

We are aware this work of virtual chaplaincy is relatively new, and we are bumping our way along. Our vision is not limited to the Tokyo Olympics, but to building a platform for future global sports events, where athletes can meet, not just during the Games, but also before and after. For access to the *Global Athletes Community*, go to our page on Facebook or Instagram.

APPENDIX A
Chapter By Chapter Application

The following is a workbook section on personal application of lessons illustrated in the book. How might God want to apply in your life some of what you read about? Each numbered exercise connects to a particular chapter:

CHAPTER ONE

The Bible greatly emphasizes God's delight in our offerings of thanksgiving as a way of life (e.g., 1 Thessalonians 5:16-18). If you think of the people who invested in your life as you were growing up, perhaps a parent, a neighbor, a teacher, a coach, or someone from church, consider writing a thank you note of appreciation.

Think of a younger person in your area who might need encouragement, and prayerfully seek a way of reaching out during the coming week (2 Timothy 2:1-2).

In this chapter I also wrote about my need to develop my athletic skills on a spiritual foundation. Is your sense of worth tied to your performance more than to who you are in Christ?

CHAPTER TWO

You have read a history of God using athletes to share His love through the sport of wrestling. Is there something you love doing, such as a hobby or a special talent, that you can use to share your faith with others?

Find a group that can encourage you in your growth as a believer.

I wrote about endurance and sacrifice. If God is calling you to a major life decision you had not been anticipating, how important is it to first count the cost, before making your commitment? (Luke 14:28-32)

CHAPTER THREE

You read of how God enabled me to realize several goals and dreams, such as meeting and marrying Noreen, traveling in North America, and being a part of the USA Olympic Team. What are *your* goals that need prayerful planning and perseverance under the power of God's favor?

I also wrote about going to the Montreal Olympics, having been conditioned with prejudice against people from the Soviet Union, and how my experience was an eye-opener. I was able to realize they are people just like anyone else. Is it possible there are similar conditionings in your own thinking toward certain people groups? If so, according to God's wisdom, how important is it to pray for those very people? (1 Timothy 2:1-4)

CHAPTER FOUR

I related my experience of winning the gold in Mexico City. That was a thrilling moment, but what does it mean now? Who talks about it anymore? The point here is very powerful and very relevant. The Bible tells us to run for the prize that won't fade. How can you apply this wisdom in your own life? (1 Corinthians 9:24-25)

I also related how Noreen and I grew together in our married life, learning about each other and what God had for our future. To be effective in our opportunities for international ministry, we had to learn that our primary identity is not in *what we do*, but in *who we are* in Christ. What ways are you seeking to strengthen your personal worth by what you do, rather than by what you have received through God's grace in Christ? (Romans 8:16-17)

CHAPTER FIVE

I wrote about a wrestling match with a man who weighed 400 pounds (180 kilograms), and how I prevailed through strategy and conditioning. Very few people will ever actually wrestle with a giant, but does your life sometimes feel like a match against something so weighty that you don't know how to deal with it? Faith in Jesus Christ, and conditioning your mind with God's Word, will enable you to prevail in even the weightiest challenges. After reading Ephesians 6:10-18, think of three things these verses say that would help you strengthen and condition your mind.

I also wrote of how God used my love of wrestling, along with Noreen's desire to be an overseas missionary, to lead us to Europe. What door is God opening for *you* to make an impact for His glory? Remember, the Great Commandment and the Great Commission start right where you are. What opportunities do you see in your neighborhood, at a local school, or as a volunteer somewhere else in the community? Remember this motto: *Pray, Go, Share.*

CHAPTER SIX

When I left the USA and had to learn the ways of life in Europe, all of the studying, working out, and moving was easier with Noreen at my side, and with teammates whom I loved and admired. Are you part of a ministry team? If not, why not? The Bible makes clear we, in Christ, are all members of a body, *"as each part does its work"* (Ephesians 4:16). Are you praying for and with your team members, encouraging them and working together?

I also wrote about the communist head coach who actually supported our work in helping his athletes build a spiritual foundation. Is there someone in your life whom you may have mistakenly assumed would not be open to a spiritual conversation? (Acts 18:9-11)

CHAPTER SEVEN

My plan to compete in the 1980 Moscow Olympics ended with the boycott, but God used that disappointment to strengthen my commitment to the larger priorities of serving His kingdom and glory. There is a Bible verse which says, *"Many are the plans in a person's heart, but it is the Lord's purpose that prevails"* (Proverbs 19:21). Do you have plans you need to give to God, trusting in His purpose? If so, what are they?

The birth of each of our children was amazing, holding in our arms a helpless little baby and feeling a love beyond words. Those experiences helped us to realize all the more how our Heavenly Father loves us beyond what we can comprehend. How much do you allow yourself to really experience your heavenly Father's loving care for you? (Matthew 7:11) Spend some time reading the following verses about God's love for you (John 1:12; Ephesians 3:16-19; 1 John 4:10).

CHAPTER EIGHT

You read about our arriving in a communist-controlled area just hours before a military lockdown was unexpectedly declared. We had a window of time for getting out, but why had God enabled us to get in before the lockdown went into effect? There are times when we might have opportunity for an easy way out of a situation, but God may have something greater in mind, and we need to listen for His directing voice. I urge you to keep this lesson in mind as you go forward in your journey. (Proverbs 3:5-7)

I also wrote of how having an Olympic champion on our team opened new doors for ministry in Europe. Not every team can have a world class athlete, but every team has some kind of talent that can be used for the Gospel. What are some of the abilities on your team, in your family, or in your church, that can be creatively used to give greater access for ministry? How can you do your part in stirring up others on your team to more fully activate their gifts from God? (Ephesians 4:16)

CHAPTER NINE

In the early 1980s, I was able to share the Good News of salvation in Christ with many people. The training I had received in sharing *The Four Spiritual Laws* of God's love, man's sin, Christ's death and resurrection, and our response, helped me to communicate this simple message in many different cultures and situations. I also wrote about unexpected opportunities for ministry in various countries. The Apostle Paul exhorted Timothy to "be prepared in season and out of season" for occasions to share (2 Timothy 4:2). It is important for us to always be ready. Do you have a simple method for telling your friends, family, and others about God's love in Christ? Check out the link to *The Four Spiritual Laws* in Appendix B.

CHAPTER TEN

In 1984, we needed to move from Vienna to a small town near Munich, just when our children were reaching school age. We had new neighbors and new teammates, but remained guided by the same vision and calling to penetrate the Soviet Bloc with the Gospel. If you move to a new neighborhood, city, or country, is God's love with the Great Commission still the guiding principle that keeps you moving forward?

I also wrote about partnering with organizations and gathering people for training. Are there opportunities for you to do something similar to this where you are? Who are the people you can do ministry with in your location? (Acts 11:25-26)

CHAPTER ELEVEN

In the 1988 fire, we faced the challenge of sudden, painful tragedy while committing our lives to the service of God. Everybody at some level faces loss and pain. How has God prepared you for spiritually and practically responding to tragedy? (2 Corinthians 6:4-10)

Also in that year, many things were rapidly changing in Eastern Europe, creating new opportunities for us to share the Gospel openly where we had to be very cautious before. To take full advantage of this opportunity among so many needy people, we gave up our comfortable home life in Germany and moved to a dark metropolis. How is God using the changes around you, and in the world in general, to position you for having a bigger impact for His kingdom? (Ephesians 2:8-10)

CHAPTER TWELVE

Moving to the Soviet Union when things were rapidly changing in Europe was a challenge with 3 young children. We knew God had called us there. In what ways might God be preparing you for major changes which require big steps of faith? (Nehemiah 1:4; Esther 4:14)

I also related how the time finally came when I simply could no longer maintain the responsibilities of family and mission work, while also keeping up the physical conditioning necessary for active athletic competition. How is God preparing you for a time when the passing of years will require major adjustments in your own life situation? (Ecclesiastes 3:1; 1 Timothy 4:7-8)

CHAPTER THIRTEEN

In the early 1990s, God was bringing a team together to help reach people in Moscow and beyond. The opportunities to provide ministry for athletes and families at all levels in sports are fantastic. How can you use your gifting and passion to serve? (Romans 12:3-13)

I related my struggles with low energy following my mountaintop experience in Barcelona. At such times, the adversary will often be poised to attack. Through God's word, we are instructed to not be ignorant of the devil's schemes, and by resisting him in the name of Christ, the adversary will flee. (2 Corinthians 2:11; 1 Peter 5:8-9) Is there a time in your life where the adversary tried to distract you from what God wanted you to do? If so, what was it?

My wife was there to do her best to understand and encourage me, and also my teammates stepped in to have a significant role. Who are the people in your life who can walk with you through the shadows? (Hebrews 10:24-25)

Although my wife and ministry partners had a crucial role in walking with me, there can be times when professional help is needed. When the time comes for a decision like that, pride can get in the way. Is there anyone in your sphere of influence or responsibility who could benefit like I did from professional Christian counseling? If so, and if there are serious obstacles, who can you bring in to help facilitate an outcome which would be best for the person in need? (1 Corinthians 12:4-5) Or, are you that person who needs to humble yourself and seek help?

CHAPTER FOURTEEN

The creativity of Taekwondo athletes using their sport to disciple others is so inspiring to me. How would God have you respond if you were told you should not use your gift or hobby as a way of reaching out to connect with people in the name of Christ? (Acts 4:18-20)

God used Noreen and I to help pioneer together with teammates in Moscow. Others came to develop and expand what we had helped to start. Who are those around you who can take your vision and make it better? (2 Timothy 2:1-2)

CHAPTER FIFTEEN

What had started as four wrestlers moving to Europe to train for the Olympics and share our faith, grew to a global partnership involving many sports teams and individuals. Every region of the world has some important sport by which many can be reached. Have you ever wondered how to use games and sports to reach kids, teens, and families in your neighborhood? For more ideas, check out ReadySetGO.world in Appendix C.

Sports conferences and ministry training were foundational for our effectiveness in expanding sports ministry throughout Eurasia and globally. Have you sought out any training opportunities where you might further develop your effectiveness for sharing the Gospel and making disciples? (Acts 18:24-26)

CHAPTER SIXTEEN

As we grew older, we experienced the pain of losing family and friends. No matter how spiritually developed any of us might become, we still have our natural emotional responses, but even in those times we are able by God's grace to not grieve without hope. (1 Thessalonians 4:13) Do you need a mentor to help motivate you and keep you accountable? If so, talk to your pastor or another spiritual leader about finding a mentor.

Learning how to grieve and mourn the loss of others raises our awareness of our own mortality, and should motivate us to take seriously the importance of mentoring the younger generation. (Psalm 90:12; Deuteronomy 6:5-7) Is there someone in your sphere of influence whom you can mentor? Develop a plan to create a deeper relationship with this person.

CHAPTER SEVENTEEN

In 2010, I was not ready to move back to the USA, but just like the move to Moscow in 1990, God directed our steps. This change gave us the opportunity to be near our grown children and other relatives, along with being reunited with Reid Lamphere (my first director with AIA in 1975). Also, the Lord used already-established relationships to open new opportunities for serving as a mentor, shepherd, and encourager at a global level. Life circumstances change, but the core values and the vision always remain the same: Loving God, loving people, and helping to make God known. What is the Lord doing to help you finish well? (Hebrews 12:1-3 and Philippians 3:12-14)

APPENDIX B
Basics of the Christian Walk

There are a few fundamentals in the Christian life that can take you from spectator to participant for the Kingdom of God. Athletes in Action has identified four basics that we believe can take your impact for Christ to the next level as you commit to learning and practicing them:

1. Articulating your Christian faith and sharing the Gospel.
2. Walking in the power of the Holy Spirit.
3. Conveying your personal story of how your life has changed.
4. Passing on what you know to equip others through discipleship.

AIA desires to help equip you for the lifelong journey of following Christ. The *Equipped* curriculum combines the best of our resources with action challenges to help you master the basic disciplines of the Christian life. We use these resources in many different settings and with many different people all around the world. You don't have to be an athlete to benefit from these resources.

For more information on AIA ministry and resources visit athletesinaction.org/resources/.

For *The Four Spiritual Laws* in other languages visit www.4laws. com/laws/languages.html

To view the JESUS film (in your preferred language) visit www. jesusfilm.org/watch.html

APPENDIX C
Ministry Organizations

Making disciples for Christ in all nations in the world of sport and play
https://readysetgo.world

ReadySetGO is the Great Commission (Matthew 28:18-20) for sports people. This website is a library of free sports ministry resources (and more) that are ready to use! It is as simple as **Ready, Set** and **GO**!

Ready is the process of gathering and envisioning people to make disciples for Christ in sport and play. **Set** prepares everyone to be a disciple-maker. **GO** gives us strategies to make disciples in the world of sport and play.

The following is a short list of Christian organizations and sports ministries which have influenced me and that I recommend. For more information on these and others, see Author's Website www.CarlDambman.com.

- **Young Life** is a Christ-centered ministry that helps kids know Jesus, grow in their faith, and serve Him.
- **InterVarsity Christian Fellowship** is a vibrant campus ministry that establishes and advances witnessing communities of students and faculty.
- **The Navigators Ministry** works around the globe to help others know Jesus and to invest in the lives of others.
- **Operation Mobilization** is a missionary organization mobilizing young people to live and share the Gospel of Jesus. Sports Link is the sports ministry of OM.

- **Youth With A Mission** equips volunteers for international ministry in a cross-cultural setting.
- **International Mission Board** takes the Good News of Jesus Christ to every corner of the world, planting churches and training pastors.
- **Fellowship of Christian Athletes** is a sports ministry whose vision is to see the world transformed by Jesus Christ through the influence of Christian coaches and athletes.
- **Missionary Athletes International** uses soccer, the world's most popular sport, to create teams that influence people for Christ.
- **Sports Friends** is a ministry of the international mission organization, SIM, which serves in more than 70 countries around the globe.
- **Ambassadors Football** partners with churches, uses football (soccer) camps, prison and school ministries, international tours, and major event ministries to share the Gospel.
- **Sports Ambassadors** exists to share the Good News, encourage the pastors and congregations, edify sports mission workers, and further equip the church. They are part of the mission OC International.
- **Christians in Sport** is a United Kingdom-based ministry that exists to reach the world of sport for Christ, working mainly with sportspeople in competitive and elite sports.
- **Sportler ruft Sportler** is a German sports organization, impacting teams and churches in Europe since 1971.

APPENDIX D
Recommended Books

Sports Ministry books which have been useful to me (for more recommendations, see Author's Website www.CarlDambman.com):

In HIS Grip, **by Greg Hicks:** The amazing adventures of AIA wrestlers from the beginning in 1967, in the US and around the world.

Muscular Christianity, **by Tony Ladd & James Mathisen:** A history of evangelical Protestants and the development of American sport.

What the book says about sport, **by Stuart Weir:** A Christian approach to sport.

Handbook on Athletic Perfection **by Wes Neal:** This book is a classic on how a Christian should compete.

Born to Play, **by Graham Daniels and Stuart Weir:** Not only can you play for Christ, you can make sport your mission.

Real Joy, **by John Ashley Null**: A tremendous resource to help athletes understand how they can experience the joy of true competition.

Front Lines, **by Roger Lipe:** A simple, direct, and applicable approach to becoming an effective sports chaplain.

Heart of a Champion, **by Roger Lipe**: A Year-Long Daily Devotional for the People of Sport.

True Competitor, **by Dan Britton and Jimmy Page**: 52 Devotions for athletes, coaches, and parents.

Heart of an Athlete, **by FCA and Matt Stover**: Daily Devotions for athletes of every level.

Uncommon, **by Tony Dungy**: Finding your path to significance, characterized by attitudes, ambitions, and allegiances that are all too rare but uncommonly rewarding.

Beyond the Gold, **by Bryan Mason**: What Every Church Needs to Know about Sports Ministry.

APPENDIX E
Freedom In Christ

I benefited greatly from the teaching ministry of Dr. Neil T. Anderson. The following outline provides verses and comments you might find helpful. For more access to similar resources, visit *Freedom in Christ Ministries* at www.ficm.org.

WHO I AM IN CHRIST

I Am Accepted

- John 1:12 – I am God's child
- John 15:15 – I am Christ's friend
- Romans 5:1 – I have been justified
- 1 Corinthians 6:17 – I am united with the Lord (one spirit)
- 1 Corinthians 6:19-20 – I am bought with a price; I belong to God
- 1 Corinthians 12:27 – I am a member of Christ's body
- Ephesians 1:1 – I am a saint
- Ephesians 1:5 – I have been adopted as God's child
- Ephesians 2:18 – I have access to God through the Holy Spirit
- Colossians 1:14 – I have been redeemed and forgiven
- Colossians 2:10 – I am complete in Christ

I Am Secure

- Romans 8:1-2 – I am free forever from condemnation
- Romans 8:28 – I am assured all works together for good
- Romans 8:31-34 – I am free from any charge against me
- Romans 8:35-39 – I cannot be separated from the love of God

- 2 Corinthians 1:21-22 – I am established, anointed, sealed by God
- Colossians 3:3 – I am hidden with Christ in God
- Philippians 1:6 – I am confident that the good work God has begun in me will be perfected
- Philippians 3:20 – I am a citizen of heaven
- 2 Timothy 1:7 – I have not been given a spirit of fear, but of power, love and a sound mind
- Hebrews 4:16 – I can find grace and mercy in time of need
- 1 John 5:18 – I am born of God; the evil one cannot touch me

I Am Significant

- Matt 5:13-14 – I am the salt and light of the earth
- Jn 15:1,5 – I am a branch of the true vine, a channel of His life
- Jn 15:16 – I have been chosen and appointed to bear fruit
- Acts 1:8 – I am a personal witness of Christ's
- 1 Cor 3:16 – I am God's temple
- 2 Cor 5:17-21 – I am a minister of reconciliation for God
- 2 Cor 6:1 – I am God's co-worker (1 Cor 3:9)
- Eph 2:6 – I am seated with Christ in the heavenly realm
- Eph 2:10 – I am God's workmanship
- Eph 3:12 – I may approach God with freedom and confidence
- Phil 4:13 – I can do all things through Christ who strengthens me

ABOUT THE AUTHOR

Carl Dambman joined Athletes In Action in 1975. He and his wife, Noreen, lived in Europe over thirty years. They moved to Vienna, Austria, with a group of AIA wrestlers training for the 1980 Moscow Olympics, and from there they helped to start sports ministry in the Soviet Bloc. Their children were born in Europe and finished high school in Moscow. Sports ministry has developed across the eleven time zones of Russia, throughout Eurasia, and around the world. They now live near Seattle, with Carl serving on AIA's Global Events Team and as an international chaplain, while also training others in sports ministry. Carl has been at 18 Summer and Winter Olympic Games. Carl and Noreen, married forty-five years, have three adult children and four grandchildren.

Printed in the United States
by Baker & Taylor Publisher Services